Hilly Laine to Hanover

a Brighton neighbourhood

Opposite: Richmond Street

CONTENTS

Overleaf: map of the Hanover area 1897

Opposite: 12 Richmond Terrace c1910

FOREWARD

This photograph of about 1870 was taken from a point on the Poor Law Institution (the Workhouse) site near the top of Elm Grove, and looks out in a north westerly direction over Lewes Road towards Round Hill and Preston. In the centre foreground is an area of small market gardens and Hanover Mill (1813-1887), standing where Bernard and Brading Roads are today. In the valley, far right, is Scabs Castle, Lewes Road viaduct and the bridge crossing Hartington Road. A few houses can be seen in Roundhill Crescent, more still in Richmond Road, with the steep flight of steps – the cat creep – connecting the two roads clearly defined. Passing down Wakefield Road to the wooded area, the isolated large houses, Sylvan Hall, Hill Lodge and Wakefield Lodge, can be identified. On the brow of the hill behind Richmond Road stands Roundhill Mill (1838-1913). On the extreme left at the top, Hamilton Road can be seen climbing above the chalk cutting of the Lovers Walk railway sheds, with below the graceful viaduct crossing London Road. St Martin's church is in the valley. The mass of small houses between Lewes Road and Upper Lewes Road are a blur in the centre.

'A Peep into the Past' by J G Bishop, Brighton Herald Office 1880
"In 1850, the area lying between Hanover Street… and Queen's Park, and between the upper part of Sussex Street and Islingwood Road, at present covered with houses, was little else than garden ground, with two windmills upon it near the Park. The Freehold Land Society's Estate, which was comprised within a triangle formed by Elm Grove, Islingword Road and Hampden Road, wholly covered by house property in 1870, was twenty years previously used as gardens."

This book – a record rather than a history – reflects the experiences of people who have lived and worked in Hanover, some in difficult circumstances. In the past, overcrowding, bad housing and poor sanitation were the lot of most people in Hanover. Many of them had moved there from areas of town where conditions were even worse. A few people have lived in Hanover all their lives. Behind some of the modernised façades lies a history of poverty that will suprise some readers.

Small red paviours or cobbles sometimes appear through the tarmac – designed to stop horses slipping; half obliterated lettering on the side of workshops, a fascia board and shop window of what is now a house, a diagonal doorway on a street corner, revealing that it was once a public house; a bigger building, once an institution, towering over a sea of small terrace houses, or a peep over a crumbling flint wall provide evidence of the history of the neighbourhood.

I first knew Hanover thirty four years ago when some of the buildings were in poor condition and lacked modern amenities. The Council made grants available for repairing the houses and providing modern facilities: bathrooms, kitchens and a hot water supply.

Hanover is still a convivial neighbourhood, but it is no longer as self-sufficient as it once was; and the horizons of its inhabitants are now very much wider than its boundaries.

Lavender Jones

HISTORY

The land beneath what is now known as 'Hanover' was once open arable fields and downland, intersected by pathways and bridleways to Lewes and Rottingdean. At the top of the hill was Tenantry Sheep Down, running up from the Level was Hilly Laine and Islingword Laine. The fields, called laines, were divided into furlongs, and subdivided for cultivation into paul pieces, which ran along the hillside to reduce erosion and soil slip. Access paths on furlong boundaries were called leakways.

The photograph below
The Central Valley from the south-east, a panorama of Brighton extending to its northern limit. The photographer was standing about half way up Richmond Street, facing west across the valley. The field to the right was part of Chate's Richmond Dairy Farm, and the house, no 34, with its roof facing the photographer, was the home of William Chate and is still there today. The backs of the houses beyond were in Liverpool Street. St Peter's church, Mocatta's Brighton station (in its original unencumbered state with the long low train shed), the railway works and St Bartholomew's church are all visible.

The small mission church built in 1866 is on the right. Fields are present on either side of the viaduct.

The Central Valley from the south-east, a panorama of Brighton

The street pattern

The streets were gradually built along the old field pattern, shown in the map on page 11. This shows Hilly Laine, the Fourth Furlong bounded by Albion Hill and Richmond Street, and Islingword Furlong bounded by Elm Grove and Islingword Road. The turnpike road at the bottom of the hill is the main road from Brighton to Lewes. The main landowners were Thomas and John Friend, Thomas Western (after whom Western Road was named and who also owned Preston Manor), the Duke of Dorset and others whose names are also remembered by streets elsewhere in the town: Sarah Boyce, Richard Tidy, Philip Mighell; and later the Whichelo family in Hanover.

By 1851 the triangular shape of land bounded by what is now Elm Grove, Queen's Park and Islingword Roads was owned by Wisdon and the Trustees of Matthew Ayes Whichelo. Much of Whichelo's land was let as arable land and the rest was market gardens. Wisdon owned much of the land between Albion Hill and Southover Street; this was still cultivated in the traditional manner by tenants who paid the annual tithe. Tamplin owned the land at the bottom of Albion Hill where the brewery was already providing employment for many local people, and where he kept three cows.

The development of Hilly Laine

Many developers found the land took a year to sell and were anxious to let it meanwhile. The small strips of land, intermingled with housing, were not of interest to farmers, so other uses such as limekilns, stables, paddocks, cowhouses and market gardens appeared. Edward Tilbury owned twenty seven perches of land, which was occupied by Obidiah Dray in 1851, and this was later to become Chate's Farm. Dray had a cowstall, yard and eight cows for which a tithe of £1.12s was paid.

A self-sufficient community

The main streets which led up the hill were occupied at an early stage by large numbers of shops, public houses, beerhouses and small industries – such as laundries, and soon there was everything the local community needed. The early census shows the diverse occupations of people in the area, many of whom came from surrounding Sussex villages and even from abroad.

1792

Landowners:

1 Thomas Kemp — 6 Pauls
2 C.S. Dickens — 2
3 T. Scutt — 3
4 Nathaniel Kemp — 5
5 Philip Mighell — 8
6 Duke of Dorset — 4
7 Thomas Kemp — 6
8 J. Hicks — 4
9 Thomas Kemp — 12
10 Nathaniel Kemp — 4
11 T. Scutt — 4
12 C.S. Dickens — 4
13 Richard L. Whichelo — 8
14 J. Hicks — 4
15 C.S. Dickens — 4
16 J. Hicks — 4
17 Duke of Dorset — 12
18 Nathaniel Kemp — 4
19 Thomas Kemp — 4
20 S. Buckoll — 4
21 T. Scutt — 10
22 Nathaniel Kemp — 2
23 Richard L. Whichelo — 8
24 Philip Mighell — 2
25 Thomas Kemp — 10
26 T. Scutt — 4
27 Thomas Kemp — 4
28 Nathaniel Kemp — 8
29 Thomas Kemp — 16
30 J. Ackerson — 4
31 C.S. Dickens — 6
32 T. Scutt — 6
33 Thomas Kemp — 12
34 Duke of Dorset — 4
35 J.C. Michell — 4
36 C.S. Dickens — 4
37 Nathaniel Kemp — 6

	Pauls
38 Thomas Kemp	4
39 J. Hicks	4
40 C.S. Dickens	8
41 Nathaniel Kemp	8
42 CS Dickens	12
43 Philip Mighell	4
44 T. Kemp	4
45 T. Scutt	4
46 Duke of Dorset	4
47 R L. Whichelo	8
48 T. Kemp	4
49 N. Kemp	4
50 C.S. Dickens	8
51 T. Kemp	4

Total 298

ROAD TO THE DOWNS

Third Furlong

SOUTHOVER STREET

ALBION HILL

Road from Lewes to Brighton

Landowners in Hilly Laine 1792

10

Map of Brighton's laines 1792

11

ALMSHOUSES

Almshouses were originally established as charitable institutions that provided care and hospitality for the poor, sick or pilgrims. In 1853 charity commissioners were appointed to control abuses in almshouses and gradually most establishments came under the control of their local authority. The Percy & Wagner Almshouses in Brighton were an example of this change of ownership.

The Percy & Wagner Almshouses were erected in the open fields north of Brighton. Was this a case of 'out-of-sight-and out-of-mind'? They were endowed at the request of Philadelphia and Dorothy Percy in 1795. The buildings are an example of the Gothick revival, but were built in two phases: the Percy Alms Houses in 1795, and the Wagner Almshouses in 1859. The first almshouses were erected by Mrs Margaret Marriot in memory of her friends Dorothea and Philadelphia Percy, the daughters of the Duke of Northumberland. These first six houses were intended for six poor widows who were members of the Church of England within the parish of Brighton,

Percy & Wagner Almshouses from a watercolour signed 'Ann Stovel 1807'

Some of these small houses were occupied by more than one person, and family members were able to live with the original occupant. Most of the women give an occupation, rather than 'Inmate of Almshouse'. The 1891 census shows all twelve of the Almshouses occupied: Prudence Davey, a widow of 69, from Hurst in Sussex, living with her granddaughter Louisa aged 11 at No 4; Selina Fuller, unmarried aged 63, from Worthing in Sussex, living with her niece Lily Louisa Shelley aged 14 at No 10. All the other houses had one resident, one with a visitor on census night. Six of the residents were single women and six were widows, only one resident was born in Brighton.

When the Reverend Henry Wagner died in 1870, he left £100 to a former servant, Jane Scrase, who was at that time resident in the almshouse. The 1901 accounts show that cloaks were purchased at Hannington's, and builders were paid for repairs. By 1903 residents were given allowances in lieu of bonnets and later in lieu of cloaks. In 1930 a sum of of £95 for the installation of gas and water to the houses was recorded. Prior to this they depended on candles, coal and a pump in the yard.

As late as 1902 a Coronation gift of £1 was given to the six widows. The women also received from Hannington's shop: two dark brown gowns, not to exceed in value 15 shillings nor less than 12 shillings; a black bonnet, not exceeding 10 shillings or under 8 shillings, once in three years; abd a Duffel cloak, not to exceed in value 21 shillings or less than 18 shillings. The residue of the income was divided amongst the inmates, and paid quarterly. In 1910 this amounted to about 4 shillings per week each.

By 1971 the almshouses were in a state of disrepair, only one was occupied and the others unfit for habitation. The Trustees wanted to demolish them, but they were listed in the same year. New kitchens and bathrooms were built in extensions at the back of the houses and the interiors redesigned, keeping the original façade.

The funds from the charity were insufficient to enable the buildings to be brought up to the required standard, so the Borough Council helped with additional money, and as a result were able to nominate tenants for nine of the twelve houses.

More recently the police box which had been built in front of the almshouses was removed; a bonus for the townscape on this traffic laden corner.

Percy & Wagner Almshouses c1970

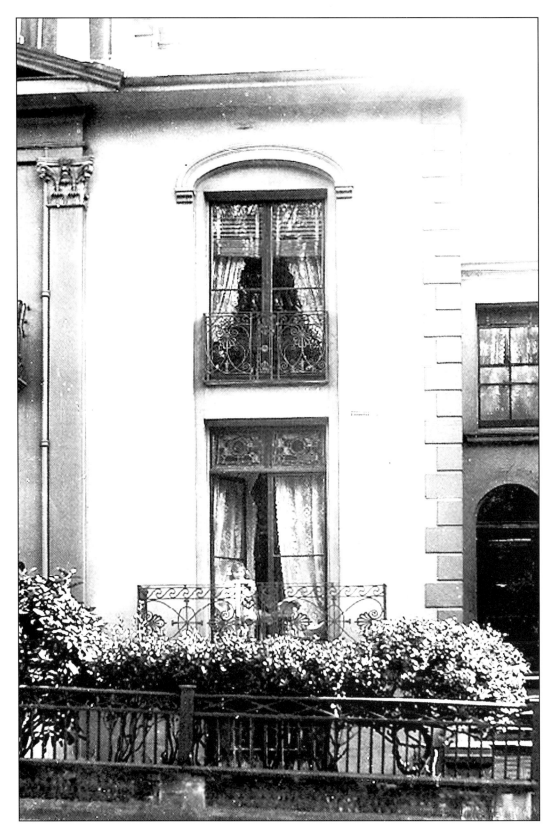

14

HANOVER CRESCENT

Carlton Hill, with its small tenement houses, abundance of public houses, workshops and slaughterhouses, had been the most northerly development until 1795, when the Percy Almshouses were built in a rural setting at the junction of Lewes Road and Race Hill Road (now Elm Grove), but by 1822 Brighton had begun to develop northwards towards the Lewes Road.

It was in the area south east of the almshouses that Henry Brooker decided to build a middle class crescent of houses. Work on the houses started in 1809 and was completed in 1821, with other substantial villas developing along the main road at the same time. In 1814 Henry Brooker employed architects Wilds and Busby to design a façade for the Crescent, with building lots being sold to individuals, enabling the rest of the house to be designed to the purchaser's own requirements.

When complete Hanover Crescent was a semicircle of 24 houses with bow fronts, shell motifs and Corinthian and Ammonite pilasters, though they were not of a uniform design. The two lodges at each end of the Crescent were single storey buildings with Tuscan columns and pediments. Title deeds describe the erection of gates 'to keep our road a private road for the exclusive use and enjoyment of the tenants and occupiers free from horse, cattle carts and other carriages'. Tenants were to pay equal amounts for the maintenance and upkeep of the grounds.

Amon Wilds lived at Richmond Lodge during the construction of the Crescent, with his builder's yard on the Level opposite his house. Charles Burchett, a builder, at 22 Richmond Buildings, whose private residence was at 1 Southover Street, was involved with the interior design of the Crescent.

Amon Wilds (1762-1833) was a builder/surveyor who had premises in the Lewes Road. He set up a business with his son Amon Henry Wilds and Charles Augustin Busby. Together they were responsible for many of Brighton's Regency squares and buildings. Amon Wilds senior, built 9 Richmond Terrace for himself and he lived there until his death in 1833. The Wilds took the ammonite as their trademark, probably as a pun on their name, and it can be seen on many of their buildings, an example of which is in the photograph of No.10 Richmond Terrace (on page 32).

The Phoenix Brewery
In 1821, just as the select development of Hanover Crescent was being completed, the Phoenix Brewery opened on land stretching from Albion Hill to Southover Street. The Level recreational area was laid out opposite the Crescent and construction of the new

Opposite: 4 Hanover Crescent c 1905

parish church of St Peter's was begun. The Crescent, a select development for middle class residents, was now in a more socially mixed neighbourhood.

Hanover Crescent initially attracted well known residents such as Horace Smith, the writer and poet, who lived at No 10 from 1826 to 1840. His house was a meeting place for the intellectual society of Brighton and among his friends were Dickens and Thackery. He was succeeded in his house by Samuel Hood, a physician, and father of the first Viscount British Admiral. So the residents of Hanover Crescent displayed some social standing.

In 1851 George Brown, a well known cricketer of the time, lived at No 10. He was the keeper of the Hanover Cricket Ground, now Park Crescent. In 1848 Roland Hill, the originator of the penny post and the chairman of the London & Brighton Railway Company, lived there. Henry Brooker himself lived at No 14 for about 20 years. John George Bishop, writer of local history and editor of the Brighton Herald, lived at No 15, which became the official residence of the Vicar of Brighton from 1839 - 1882. When the house was sold it was combined with No 9 to make Hanover House, which became St Paul's Convent School run by a Mother Superior from Belgium. Professional, middle class people inhabited the Crescent, a contrast with the rest of Hanover.

Charles Hammond brought No 18 Hanover Crescent in 1824, but his stay was short lived as he was declared bankrupt and the property sold at auction on the premises on 13 April 1826. The description of the contents gives an insight into the furnishings of that time:

> **The list of contents of 18 Hanover Crescent**
> "All the handsome and modern household furniture; consisting of lofty four post bedsteads with carved mahogany pillars, and tastefully arranged chintz and dimity furniture; large sized and well seasoned goose feathered beds; hair and wool mattresses; Witney blankets and counterpanes; capital mahogany chests of drawers, night commodes, basin stands, dressing, Pembroke, card, dining and claw tables; handsome Brussels carpets; large size chimney, pier and dressing glasses; stuffed horse hair sofa with rich chintz furniture; mahogany and japanned chairs; half-tester bedstead, with neat printed furniture etc; an assortment of plate and linen; a quantity of oil cloth and Venetian stair carpeting; together with a general collection of kitchenware."

Mr Smith Hannington of the drapery trade left his house in Hanover Crescent to Mr Samuel Hannington in 1826; later it was occupied by an accountant of Hannington's (a well-known department store in North Street which closed a few years ago). No 19 was bought by the Brighton Co-operative Society in 1929, which they extended at the rear to form a dairy, supplying milk to the area until the 1990s.

The 1851 Census for Hanover Crescent

One house had only a maid in residence and therefore only 22 households had a head of household. Of the 22 heads of households 10 were married men, three widowers, two widows, six single females and one unmarried female. No females were marked on the census as having an occupation other than fundholders, annuitant and a retired governess.

Some of the residents of Hanover Crescent appear in the Court Directory, indicating a certain wealth and standing. Of the 22 heads of household none were born in Sussex, most of the heads of household were retired or fundholders, so they did not have to earn a living and were therefore able to live on the edge of the town. Each family had at least two servants and possibly had other staff who lived out, as several women in nearby Hanover Street and Hanover Terrace state their profession as housemaids.

Henry Brooker, the original developer of Hanover Crescent, also commissioned a small street of houses to be built (in 1822) directly behind it, to be called Hanover Street, which included a completely different social mix (as shown in the census details, page 19) in contrast to the grand middle class houses in the Crescent.

> **Advertisement from The Brighton Gazette 20 June 1822**
> "To be Let – on building leases with purchasing clauses. A very Eligible Freehold Ground at the back of Hanover Crescent. Intended to form a street, and houses to be set back 14' on each side of the street, to form forecourts or garden plots for each tenement, so that the distance between the houses will be 58'. Roads about 10' wide at each end of the street are intended to be made from the Lewes Road to Hanover Street. For particulars apply to Mr Penfold, Solicitor, Princes Place or to Mr A H Wilds, Builder, Level, Brighton."

Hanover Crescent, showing the bare hills of Hilly Laine

HANOVER STREET

Damaged street sign carved into the wall of a house in Hanover Street

A map c1822 shows the planned Hanover Street running behind the Crescent before construction had started, but in Baxter's Strangers' Guide of 1824, Hanover Street is listed as small tenements. The houses were tiny, some two, some three storeys, built piecemeal with no uniform design, with large pieces of land remaining undeveloped for years.

Indentures relating to Nos 73-74 Hanover Street show that a Mr William Penfold the younger, living at 71 Middle Street, purchased a piece of land to the west of Hanover Street which he left to his wife Mary on his death in 1868. In 1873 Mary Penfold left the house to John Croucher Penfold, a solicitor, who sold the property to Walter Boniface for £115 in 1877. Mr Boniface lent £150 to Mr Albert Henry Wilson, coal merchant, so that he could purchase the property from him. By May 1878 Mr Wilson had paid back the loan and owned the property, which, with the house and the land next to it, were used for his coal business.

Nos 73 and 74 Hanover Street

In 1891 Albert Wilson, a coal merchant from Midhurst, lived at No 73 with his wife Martha, a daughter and a cousin who was a servant. No 74 was used as a coal shed. Arthur, son of Albert Wilson, sold the house in 1914 to William Thomas Bradshaw, Auctioneer's Clerk, for £230, £100 of this repaired to Anna Alice Bates, widow, who had loaned Albert Wilson money. Later that year William Bradshaw sold the house to Albertina Maud Mathias for £250, whom he married a month later, an astute move on his part!

No 73 continued to be used as a coal merchant's house from time to time until the 1930s. Mrs Bradshaw gave the house to Thomas Alfred Tillman in a deed of gift in 1957. He had been the chauffeur to William Bradshaw and was also head projectionist at the Duke of York's cinema. He lived there with his large family of twelve children, cooking on a range set into a chimney breast and bathing in a tin bath in front of the fire. His son, took over joint ownership with his wife in 1988 and sold the house in 1991, the first time the house had been sold for 77 years.

1851 Census
Of the 24 houses in Hanover Street on census night, 30 March 1851, 23 were occupied and one was empty.

Hanover Street had forty five dwellings registered on census night in 1851, which included sixty eight heads of household. Some of the houses had two or three different families living in them, possibly one on each floor. Overcrowding was rife.

The census shows that the majority of the heads of household in Hanover Street were from Sussex, but outside Brighton, probably attracted to the town with the prospect of obtaining work. Most were unskilled and had possibly previously worked on farms. Unlike the heads of household in Hanover Crescent, few came from the London area, but sixteen of the sixty eight came from other counties.

The occupants of Hanover Street included: nineteen labourers, a sailor and a Chelsea pensioner. Of the heads of households eleven were women, nine of whom were laundresses, one a needlewoman and one an English teacher. Of the nine laundresses, seven were widows, one married and one single.

Much of the open land above Hanover Crescent was used as drying fields for laundries. In all there were twenty women in Hanover Street involved in laundry work including three ironers. The women without a husband to support them would have had a hard life relying on hand washing for their income.

> **In 1864 an observer remembered what the area used to be like:**
> There were only a few houses scattered here and there, among the market gardens, made on the side of what once formed part of the Brighton Downs. Now there are sixteen streets of small, modern houses for artisans; eight streets in parallel lines, intersected by the upward road. Two streets are occupied by small shopkeepers of various trades.
>
> At one o'clock the streets are thronged by men returning from the station works for their dinner; this shows the occupation of many of the inhabitants. Others are employed in various houses of business, or do shop work at home. There are also a great number of small laundries: with the exception of the bottom row of houses facing the main road [Hanover Crescent] which are of a somewhat superior kind, the whole parish is essentially poor.

The Hollow

A twitten runs between Hanover Street and Hanover Terrace and is known locally as 'The Hollow'. There used to be a public house 'The Little Fox' on one corner and a shop on the other, the overhanging fascia boards are evidence of their former use.

In 1976 the twitten was threatened with a stopping up order by Brighton Council, as they had received a petition from eighty three local residents calling for its closure as it was being misused by local children. Two days before the Highways and Transport Committee of the Council applied to the court for a closure order another group of residents submitted a counter-petition with ninety two signatures.

. . . [the twitten] was a great help to the elderly and disabled and one of them were nearly in tears when she thought it would be closed.
Betty Parker

The 156 year old twitten was of historic interest and should be preserved.
Robert Gregory : the then chairman of the Brighton Society

The twitten remains open to this day. Hanover Street is more varied than other Hanover streets in character, height and design, and in 1988 it was added to the Valley Gardens conservation area.

PUBLIC BATHS

Houses in Hanover were not built with bathrooms, so public baths were an essential facility for the community, and also served as a popular meeting places for bathers. Cobden Road public slipper baths were opened in April 1894 by Sir Joseph Ewart, the Mayor, after whom Ewart Street is named. It is a red brick building with shell and dolphin decorations at the corners and separate entrances for women and men.

When Hanover was designated an Improvement Area in the 1970s, bathrooms were installed in many of the houses for the first time and demand for the public baths fell. Cobden Road Baths were closed in 1976 and the building was used as the Hanover Community Centre until 1982, then as a resource centre until its conversion into flats in 1985-86. The conversion kept the façade, and the inaugural tablet still remains in the entrance hall.

I lived in Islingword Road in the 1920s and 30s and used Cobden Road Baths. Mr and Mrs Gillam and their daughter Eileen ran the baths at the time. I went every week, it was two pence for a bath, three pence for a towel.
G Hayward

On Saturdays I would met up with friends and go to the wonderful Cobden Road Baths. The water was deep and we would call out "more hot in number five please" in order to keep the water temperature up.
Susan Davies

My father worked for the Brighton Council Waterworks division and was therefore involved with Cobden Road baths and looked after the big piece of ground between the resevoir wall and the back of the old soup kitchen. The building fronting Cobden Road was a very old one-storey Victorian building which always looked very ramshackle and had a funny smell to it. The baths were sold by Brighton Corporation in the 1980s and Southern Water now control the water works, so it has all changed. The old cottage on the site was demolished in the 1950s and nothing has been built on there since.
Walter Hope

The Cobden Road Baths included six second class baths for men and four for women, three first class baths for men and two for women.

Ground and first floor plans of the Cobden Road Slipper Baths

Opposite: the façade of Cobden Road baths with separate entrances for men and women

INSTITUTIONS

The Home for Penitent Females was erected in Finsbury Road in 1870 at the expense of the Reverend George Wagner. It provided a refuge for girls considered to be 'in moral danger', but gradually changed to accept unmarried pregnant women and girls, who had to work in the laundry attached to the Home. In 1918 it was closed owing to lack of funds, but was opened the following year as the Albion Church Army Home for Girls. By 1947 was known as the Church Army Maternity and Child Welfare Home. It was demolished in 1958.

People's Magazine, 1 July 1899 – 'Work Among the Lost' by the author of 'Home Thoughts for Working Women and Mothers' Meetings'.
George Wagner, who, having been ordained had taken the district church of St Stephen's Brighton [formerly on the corner of Canning Street and Sutherland Road], was walking down one of the back streets of that place, when three girls, with no bonnets on their heads, passed in front of him, talking in loud coarse tones, and laughing wildly with 'that laughter that is not mirth'. At once he felt that they were outcasts from God and men, yet with immortal souls, capable of being redeemed, capable of 'shining as the stars for ever and ever'. At once a forgotten sermon rushed into his mind – the sense that he was responsible for them and for thousands like them if he made no effort to save them; and in a moment the buried seed of ten years sprang to life.

. . . George Wagner and Mrs Vicars worked for three months. . . rescued 30 girls and took them to London to various refuges, but when the London refuges couldn't take any more it became necessary that a home should be provided in Brighton. An appeal was made and quickly responded to … a small house opposite the Level was taken and 15 penitents were also lodged in a larger house on the Lewes Road.

[The] building which stands on one of the hills immediately behind Brighton, [is] known by the name of the Albion Hill Home for Female Penitents. A pretty building, it is bright and pleasant to look at, set round with its glossy evergreens, and overlooking the valley below, spanned by its noble viaduct, and the distant hills breathing in their blue tranquillity.

…The building itself is bright and pleasant to the eye, and as you enter, you are shown into large, bright, airy rooms, the walls are hung with bright pictures, and pretty illuminated texts; floods of sunshine stream in at the large window; no vexatious inflictions, such as cutting the hair short, are in force; the common dress of the institution differs little from that of an ordinary servant; and

24

remembering that the inmates come fresh from the wild license of an uncontrolled life, the monotony of the day's work is broken by being turned out for an hour's good play in the garden in summer, with swings, skipping ropes, gardening and all kinds of games in full force; while in winter they are supplied with quiet indoor games and amusements. They are not encouraged to make much profession of religion while in the Home, nor is attendance at many religious services exacted from them.

. . . The daily rules of the Albion Hill Home are that the inmates rise at 5.30 am in summer and 6.30 am in winter, and work until 8 pm, being allowed an hour for dinner, and half an hour for their other meals . . . they are allowed an hour for recreation from 8 pm until 9 pm. Simple instruction is given three times a week, in reading, writing and summing; but the attendance is more or less optional, though most take advantage of it. On Sunday they go to church in the morning, but in the afternoon a service is held in their own little chapel by the chaplain.

A girl on being admitted is placed at once on the probationers' ward [with] the private laundry, where all the washing of the Home itself is done, so that she learns the whole business of washing, ironing and getting up on the clothes belonging to the institution. Thence she passes, a tolerably practised hand, into the public laundry, by which arrangement the Institution is enabled to take in washing for a higher class than can usually be done by inexperienced hands, and to turn out the best laundry work, nearly £1,000 being annually made by washing and needlework combined. The Home also had the idea that using physical strength worked off unhealthy thoughts and the girls enjoyed the face to face contact with other girls. Having thoroughly learnt the work of the laundry, the girl passes into the kitchen, where she is taught the duties of a kitchen maid; and thence she passes finally into the workroom, where she is trained in needlework and the use of the sewing machine.

The girls are carefully taught to feel that the Home is not a prison house – that at any time they demand the old clothes they came in and, persuasion proving useless to induce them to stay, they may take their departure. But those who hope to obtain a situation are expected to remain in training two years. . . at the end of which time a complete outfit of clothes is given to them, a Bible, a Prayer Book, and a writing case, and they are placed in an eligible situation, a gift of 10 shillings being given to them if they keep it for a year. This they seldom fail to claim; and thus the way is open before them to a [more] respectable, happy and useful life.

The 1871 census indicates ten members of staff: a matron and her assistant, a wash house supervisor, a laundry matron and her assistant, a housekeeper and her husband, a carpenter, a probation matron and a monitor; and 61 inmates: the youngest – Elizabeth Avery – aged 11 from Brighton, and the oldest – Charlotte Hayner – a widow aged 41 from Middlesex. Of the 61 inmates only 20 came from Brighton. There were four pairs of sisters including May and Harriet Yates from Brighton, aged 14 and 13.

In 1881 there were 14 staff and 48 girls between the ages of 15 and 19, their occupations were mostly laundry and kitchen maids. One of them was a Mary Waas aged 18, occupation needlewoman, born in Rotterdam, Holland. By 1891 there were 8 staff and 36 inmates, many of whom came from other parts of the country, and by 1894 there was accommodation for 80 inmates.

Brighton Home for Penitent Females

During 1911, 120 girls were living at the institution, 40 having left, 32 of whom had been sent into service, ten were returned to friends and six left of their own will, of whom three were subsequently re-admitted, leaving seventy two girls on the roll on 31st December. The annual report shows that circumstances, outwardly anyway, may have improved since the seemingly draconian regime of the home in the previous century.

Gratuities of 10s each were awarded to eight girls who kept their first situation for 12 months. Kind and loving treatment, regular hours for active employment, systematic Bible teaching, moral and useful instruction under the superintendence of the chaplain, Mrs MacDonald, and the efficient matron and her staff, who exercise loving tact, wise and firm control and enduring patience – all these have had the effect of transforming character to such a large degree as to surpass the hopes of the most sanguine.

The character of the education given in the present day was thought to be another cause. Young people needed the kind of education that was formerly in the good old parochial schools; he felt the want of religious instruction caused many to err.

The Reverend A E Wynne, the then vicar of Rottingdean . . . also referred to the overcrowding, which he said prevailed not only in towns, but in the country as well. He hoped for much from the Housing and Town Planning Act. A great deal of evil they were fighting against was caused by a certain amount of feeble-mindedness in girls. He praised the work done in Brighton as really great, noble and useful.

The Coronation of George V on 23 June 1911 was cause for celebration and the day was observed as a holiday in the Home. The Committee gave a grant of £5 towards the festivities and after a thanksgiving service in the chapel, each girl was presented with a Coronation Testament, a framed card and a medal. There were 'suitable' decorations in and outside the buildings, and in the evening Chinese lanterns and fairy lights added to the festive appearance; which must have illuminated what was normally a rather gloomy Victorian building.

> **Extract from a letter published as an advertisement for the Home. Letter from Mistresses:**
> "I have had three or four girls from the Home, and they have turned out good servants and have done well. I have a girl now in my service, I had a little trouble with her at first, but she is now a very steady, good girl, and a capital, hardworking servant."

In 1916, during the First World War, my mother had my eldest sister in the Finsbury Road Home. She was unmarried and the father of the child was in the army. Mother had 12 brothers and sisters, but not one of them offered to help her. She stayed at the home for most of her pregnancy, although she was very unhappy there. The girls slept in dormitories, and during the day had to scrub the stone floors and work in the laundry. Although she had not received much support from her family in the beginning, my grandmother offered to look after her daughter after she was born, instead of her being sent to an orphanage, as most of the babies were. My grandmother lived in a small cottage in Patcham village and for five happy years my sister lived there with her. Unfortunately my grandmother died when my sister was five and she was then fostered for a year until my mother married and was able to look after her herself. My father accepted my sister as his own, my sister idolised him, she could never tell that she was not his child and was shocked when she found out.

Patricia Sprinthall

I attended Finsbury Road Infants and Junior school until I was 14. Opposite the school was the Church Army Home for unmarried mothers run by several Sisters from the Church Army. Every morning when all the children were at school, the girls were taken out in groups of about 12 for a walk in Queen's Park. They were not pitied, most people thought that they had made their own beds and had to lie on them, but many of the girls had been slung out of home. Most of the babies were adopted. The girls were kept away from the children in the school because they thought that we would 'barrack' them.

G Harwood

I lived at 11 Queen's Park Road in the late 1930s; on Sunday mornings at 9.40 am a crocodile of 20 or more girls would walk down the road to morning service at St Mary's Kemp Town, two very stern nuns in the front, and two more at the rear. All the girls had scrubbed, red – perhaps with embarrassment – faces, and the clothes stretched tight across their stomachs – no maternity clothes in those days. Upon hearing the marching feet mother would come out and call my sister and me in from the little front courtyard where we were playing saying "Quickly, here come the naughty girls", and in we would go. The same thing happened when they all marched back on the other side of the road. I'm not sure if I realised why they were called 'the naughty girls', but remember thinking how young and poor some of them were.

June Marshall

Two ladies in Montreal Road also looked after girls who were pregnant. The girls were paid for privately by their families and the girls would return home after the birth and the babies would be adopted. The ladies adopted two of the children.
Olive Denman

I lived opposite the Home for Unmarried Mothers for 30 years and when I was in the Junior School the matron used to let me go over and bath the babies.

J Fennel

The story of the Home for Penitent Females is poignant, and seems almost unbelievable today. In the past if a single girl had a baby it lowered the social standing of her extended family. However Olive Denman's and J Fennel's recollections show that there was some concern for the inmates of the Home and their offspring, at least by a few local people.

'The Story of Bevan Funnell Ltd' by Pamela Bevan Funnell and 'Brighton Ghosts' by Frank Usher

The harsh poor laws and the unfeeling treatment of unmarried mothers caused untold suffering and unhappiness. Many were probably glad to see the building pulled down, but it remained empty for many years and the council was hard put to find a suitable tenant. A large Gothic building with a floor area of 12,000 square feet, it was not suitable for many businesses, but in 1952 the building was leased to furniture manufacturer Bevan Funnell Ltd. Machinery was stored in the basement, offices were on the ground floor, a polishing shop on the first floor, and the chapel was used as the despatch department. Forty staff were employed, their ages ranging from 15-50.

Mrs Bevan occupied what had been the matron's office, together with her mother and a part-timer who did filing, etc. Mr Funnell was at that time a member of the Hove Borough Council and became Mayor of Hove in 1960. He was also a special Constable, and both he and his wife were practical, matter-of-fact, business people. The Bevan family also had a mongrel dog called Blarney, who accompanied them to the factory every day.

Then strange, unexplained things started to happen. The police warned the Bevans that the doors to the building were found unlocked at night. This was strange, as the caretaker who lived on he premises made sure the building was secure, but even padlocked doors were found to be unlocked. Furniture would be turned over and chairs moved, but little damage could be found.

The one evening as it was getting dark, a driver was working in the packing room on he first floor. Turning, he saw a woman standing in the doorway dressed in a black suit; as he spoke to her, she disappeared. He ran to the door and up the passage, but there was no sign of her; he came down the stairs and related what he had seen, but the others made light of it.

Shortly afterwards Mrs Bevan was working late one night, as she often did, Blarney the dog at her side. She noticed later that he was missing and became aware of him whimpering on the first floor above the office. She went upstairs to see what was wrong and entered the long room which had been divided down the middle many years ago by a sliding partition. The Bevans were using it as a storeroom and had been unable to move the divider as it was rusted solid. As Mrs Bevan opened the door she noticed the divider had been moved across the room without a sound to the office below. The dog was trapped behind the partition. Mrs Bevan ran downstairs calling to the men who were loading a van, who ran back with her and together managed to push the partition enough to get the dog out. It remained immoveable after that.

The Funnells and their staff were convinced that the building was haunted. They began to make inquiries about its history and discovered it had been a home for unmarried mothers. In Victorian times such institutions were often grim places run on penal lines.

In the centre of the building was a small room the Bevans used as an office. Across the passage was a cloakroom and lavatory. One day in the passage a strong perfume could be smelt by all the staff. Mrs Funnell described it as a musky smell almost like incense, but peculiarly feminine and sensuous. Sometimes the perfume would seem to blow in waves around the building; no one could ever discover its origins. One day a heavily knitted cardigan in black wool appeared mysteriously in the cloakroom. It was hanging on a peg and was deeply impregnated with this strange perfume. No one owned it, and a day or two later it disappeared and was never seen hanging there again. The Funnells suspected they were being subjected to tricks being played upon them by someone wanting them to vacate the building, but even if this was so, some of the things that happened were inexplicable.

The typewriter in the office would be heard typing furiously when no one was in the room. When the door was opened the noise stopped. As was to be expected, the Funnells had problems with the staff over the haunting. Many of them were scared off, others laughed at the idea of ghosts and others stuck it out of loyalty to the firm.

In 1953, a year after the Funnells took over the building, some local spiritualists held a séance there. Mrs Funnell attended this séance, during which a girl was supposedly contacted, speaking in a Sussex accent she said, "Matron is cruel to me, I am desperately unhappy; I've tried to be good, but I can't." "She sounded a miserable little thing", said Mrs Funnell. The Funnells were sceptical about this séance.

Nevertheless, a strange thing happened immediately after the séance had finished. As soon as the spiritualists had left, there was a tremendous noise of people running all over the building, of doors banging, people calling and of pounding footsteps, followed by silence. This silence lasted until the Sunday before Christmas 1954, when Mr Funnell went to the office by himself to catch up with a backlog of work. By then the past happenings had been forgotten and he was only concerned with the rush of Christmas orders. It was a bright December day. As he went into the office he heard a thud, as though a book had been dropped. He looked along the built-in bench around the walls, and what he saw haunted him for the rest of his life.

Appearing through one of the benches was a human figure. The bench could be seen through it and it seemed to turn towards Mr Funnell. As it slowly turned he could see what he described as 'a face shape with eyes'. The feeling he had was that someone was looking at him with incredible hatred and loathing, which filled him with overwhelming fear. He fled from the room and out of the building. "I felt waves of hate coming at me and I was utterly terrified," he said as he described later to his wife what he had seen.

He returned at lunchtime ashen, his eyes sunken and it was many hours before he recovered himself. Mr Funnell was so shaken by this experience that he decided to obtain the services of a priest to come and exorcise the premises. They found a local man who arranged an exorcism, after which they had no more trouble from hauntings.

A few years later the Funnells left the building and it was immediately demolished by the Council, who quickly built a block of flats on the site. The Funnells heard later that the occupants of the flat which would have been in the part of the building where the supposed hauntings had been, complained to the Council that they were continually having trouble with drafts, windows opening, noises, doors thrown open, books thrown around and so on. So it would seem there may have been more than one troubled spirit, judging by the uproar sometimes heard.

The Northern Branch of the Lying-In Institute

'Clydesdale', formerly North Lodge at 10 Richmond Terrace, was built in 1849, and described in the earliest conveyance as a large house and coach house built for Amon Henry Wilds in the 5th furlong of Hilly Laine. It remained a private house until 1898 when it became the Northern branch of the Lying-In Institution and Hospital. The only maternity hospital in Sussex, it was funded by subscribers, who were entitled to recommend patients.

It provided lying-in wards for normal deliveries, hospital wards for difficult births and other gynaecological cases, as well as a dispensary for out-patients, and a domiciliary midwifery service.

Clydesdale, formerly North Lodge, 10 Richmond Terrace c1905

Brighton and Hove Hospital for Women.

No. 6   Date 4-5-10   Registered No. 245

Name M? Peacock   Aged 23

Address 8 Buk St

Jones

When the Midwife's assistance is required, this Card must be sent to

10 RICHMOND TERRACE.

When the House Surgeon's assistance is required at any time during the MONTH AFTER DELIVERY, Notice, together with this Card, must be sent, BEFORE 9.30 A.M., to

76 WEST STREET.

1.—The Midwife must be summoned immediately on the commencement of labour.

2.—If through neglect of Rule 1 the child be born before the arrival of the Midwife, the patient will forfeit her right to attendance, and no fees paid will be refunded.

3.—No examination of the patient by persons unconnected with the Hospital is allowed.

Infringement of these Rules forfeits the right to all attendance.

Patients are required to give IMMEDIATE NOTICE of any case of TYPHOID FEVER, SCARLET FEVER, MEASLES, SMALL POX, DIPHTHERIA, GERMAN MEASLES or ERYSIPELAS occurring in the house or their family within two months of the expected confinement. The Institution will not undertake to attend the labour if notice of such infectious disease has not been so given.

5000—12/07.

Notice of expected confinement at the Brighton and Hove hospital for women in 1910

This was one of the forerunners of the town's hospitals, which were benevolent and charitable institutions established in the 19th century, mainly for the benefit of the poor.

The Lewes Road Dispensary for Women & Children opened on 31st October 1899 at 145 Islingword Road. Its aim was 'To afford poor women of Brighton and the neighbourhood the opportunity of free consultation with doctors of their own sex'.

In 1903 the Lying-in-Institute at 76 West Street and 10 Richmond Terrace treated 126 in-patients requiring operations, 966 confinement cases in their own homes, and 798 out-patients were prescribed for.

The Lying-in Institute remained at Clydesdale until 1906 when the building became part of the Municipal Technical College and the Brighton & Hove Hospital for Women moved to number 8 Richmond Terrace (formerly the home of the Attree family). It remained at this address until 1927 when it closed and the building became another annexe of the Municipal Technical College.

CHURCHES AND CHAPELS

Religion played a major part in Brighton's affairs. As attitudes towards opposing denominations eased so chapels of various sects were built in the town.

Many of the pews were rented to wealthy worshippers to provide an income for their ministers, while poor people had to crowd into the old parish church, St Nicholas, and the few free sittings which were available. It was to remedy this situation that Henry and Arthur Wagner embarked, at great personal expense, on a massive church building scheme from the 1830s until the 1870s. It was not until the 1900s that the passionate feeling between High and Low Church in the town died down. The church of the Annunciation is one of the Wagner churches, and, like many churches in the town, it established an elementary day school for poor children in addition to a Sunday school.

The Church of the Annunciation

The Church of the Annunciation, between Washington Street and Coleman Street, was designed and built by William Dancy in 1864, with additions by Edmund Scott in 1881. The Reverend Arthur Douglas Wagner saw the workers' cottages springing up amongst the market gardens on the hill in the 1850s and was determined to build a church in the area. The fashionable Brighton churches drew crowds and charged pew rents, but this church was to be a place which was free and devoted only to its immediate neighbourhood.

The interior of the Church of the Annunciation

The church was opened on 15 August 1864, The Feast of The Assumption. A school for girls and infants was originally provided below the church, open to the air on three sides. In 1865 plans were lodged for the building of a boys' school in Southover Street. It was intended that once the school for girls had been built, that the normal east west axis of the church would be restored, ie the floor removed and the altar placed at the Washington Street end. When the parish was consulted, they preferred the present simple lines and so the liturgical south aisle and the Holy Name Chapel were added in 1881.

The Annunciation window above the high altar was given to the church in memory of Elizabeth Austin Attree, the first parishioner of the new church, wife of George Attree, who died in 1865, and whose family owned much of the land in the area. The window was designed by Edward Burne-Jones and executed by William Morris.

The first priests were the Reverend Charles Anderson, the Reverend Christopher Thompson – who stayed until 1875 and began the Sunday School, choir and the use of vestments – and Father George Chapman. Chapman was born in Liverpool in 1864 and arrived in Brighton to take up the post as priest at the Church of Annunciation in 1877, living at 85 Coleman Street. It must have been a very different living from that of his last parish of St James-the-Less in Liverpool, with about 10,000 parishioners of every European nationality, and well-nigh every religious denomination. Chapman was well thought of in the parish of Hanover, and highly respected by other clergy of the town because of his abilities as an evangelist, but he provoked antagonism among the town's low church faction by his extreme ritualism and love of Romish detail. His style of preaching was different from other Anglo-Catholic churches in Brighton and he actively discouraged middle class 'carriage folk' from visiting his church. Protestant protesters kept away from this very deprived area of town not wishing to tangle with the 'rough' element of the area.

The dissenting minister, who had a chapel on the hill, said that the parish had a totally different appearance after Father Chapman had been there some time and showed his reverence by bringing a wealth of flowers to the church on the day of his funeral.

An observer at the time recalls . . .
Within half an hour's walk of the fashionable parts of Brighton, halfway up a steep hill from the Lewes Road, stands the Church of The Annunciation. The parish is compact, no house within it being more than five minutes walk from the church. Fifty years ago there were only a few houses scattered here and there among the market gardens, made on the side of what once formed part of the Brighton Downs. Now there are 16 streets of small, modern houses for artisans; eight streets lie in parallel lines, intersected by the upward road. Many of the houses contain two or more families, while more than one of them are occupied by ladies who devote themselves to work amongst the poorer brothers and sisters.

There was one occasion, however, when some local people resorted to violence. The clergy and choir attempting to walk in procession through the parish were mobbed and an attempt was made to burn them by setting their surplices on fire.

Father Chapman died in 1891 of tuberculosis, aged only 44. It was difficult for anyone who was present at his funeral, and who witnessed the reverend order of the dense crowd collected on that day, to believe the violence that had occurred on that eventful day some 14 years previously. He was succeeded by the Reverend Reginald Fison, who carried on the good work of his predecessor, dying of typhoid in 1895 aged 42.

Aubrey Beardsley the artist, and his sister Mabel, chose to worship at the Church of the Annunciation whilst living in Lower Rock Gardens. Beardsley forged a close bond with Father Chapman who became a father figure to him in the absence of his own. The Anglo-Catholic ritualistic ceremonies were to have a profound effect on Beardsley, who later became a Roman Catholic.

In 1898 The Archbishop of Canterbury declared the use of incense and portable lights within services to be illegal, and many clergy complied with this. The Annunciation was one of the few churches in Brighton where this prohibition was ignored.

Belgrave Street Congregational Chapel

Belgrave Street Congregational Chapel was built in the Early English style by Thomas Simpson, rendered, with a pitched roof and large windows, and was erected by voluntary subscription. It opened in 1863, with a class room and reading room added for the Brighton Working men's Union, but closed in 1942 when it became an annexe to the Technical College. At one time it was used by the University of Brighton as a sculpture studio, but in 1999 permission was granted to convert it to housing.

Elevation of Belgrave Street Congregational chapel facing Belgrave Street

"A Place of Worship, part of which would be used as Day and Sunday School… within a radius of about five hundred yards … were then residing more than two thousand families… nearly all of them being mechanics or day labourers… the building would principally be for the working classes… the population is still rapidly increasing."

The infants' schoolroom was opened for public worship in 1859, the chapel and new schoolroom were opened in 1863.

"The chapel is divided from the school room by very large doors, removable at will, being on wheels – so as to throw all the building into one."

Bentham Road Mission

Bentham Road Congregational Mission Hall opened in 1882 and became a Free Church in the late 1950s; it closed in the late 1980s.

I come from a family of seven and attended the Mission with my brothers and sisters between 1935 and 1937. You entered at the front of the building and to your right were stairs leading to a balcony. You walked through a doorway and you were in a large hall where all the services were held, including the children's Sunday School. The boys and girls sat at opposite sides of the hall on oak forms arranged in a square, with a teacher for different age groups. The forms were arranged in rows across the hall when we gathered together for general assembly, for the Sunday evening meetings for adults, harvest festivals, magic lantern shows and various other events.

There was an organ which one of the teachers played whilst working a pedal. Around the walls hung framed texts on a white background with blue lettering, and two marble plaques. Standing either side of the hall were two large round cast iron stoves, which in winter were very welcome.

Passing through the main hall there was a door which led to a smaller hall where the younger children were taught, also meetings of the Girls' Guildry, Girls' Life Brigade and Boys' Brigade. Adjacent to this hall was a passage way leading to a small flight of stairs leading to a small room which was used for a Bible class. It was opened as an infant school in 1896. We had a Sunday School outing to Burgess Hill, the highlight of the year. There were quite a few church halls and missions in the Hanover area run by benevolent people who fulfilled a need for the poor of that time.
F E Smith and P Brooker

Ebenezer Baptist Chapel, Richmond Street in 1960

Ebenezer Baptist Chapel

The Ebenezer Baptist chapel, a Renaissance style building opened in 1825, in Richmond Street, on the corner of Cambridge Street, and was known as the Lemon Squeezer. It was demolished in 1966 and the replacement, by C J Wood, still stands in Richmond Parade, though it has been vandalised by squatters. In 2007 permission was granted for its demolition and replacement with a new church and 49 flats.

I attended the Ebenezer Chapel Sunday School in Richmond Street and occasionally St Peter's Church. We were Church of England but the Ebenezer was nearer to our house. If you attended regularly you got points towards the summer outing which was usually to Victoria Gardens in Burgess Hill or to Hassocks. Pastor Kemp was in charge of us and Mr Spooner the caretaker also came. At Victoria Gardens there was a coconut shy and we would ask 'Daddy' Spooner, as he was known, to take our turn because he was so good. The people at the Ebenezer were very kind to the poor in the area, they would loan you a clean blanket for one shilling and you could keep it all winter; when you returned it you could get your shilling back and they would wash it ready for next year. My family didn't have to do that as we were fairly well off compared to many in the neighbourhood.
Connie Dowds

Islingword Road Mission

The Trustees of the Primitive Methodist Church bought the plot of land in Islingword Road in 1881 and built an iron church. They sold it in 1892 and the Islingword Road Mission opened in 1893. Five years later the building was found to be dangerous and services were transferred to Finsbury Road School and the building rebuilt. The first service held in the new building was in 1899. In 1990 the name 'Mission' was felt to be old fashioned and it was called 'Islingword Road Evangelical Free Church'. The building celebrated its centenary in 1999, but was burnt down shortly afterwards. A block of flats called 'Emmanuel House' has now been erected on the site.

Islingword Road Mission Outing 1912

I was taken to the Mission by my parents over 80 years ago when just a baby. No one who went to the Mission will ever forget the summer and winter treats. They were a triumph of organisation with Mr Groves at the helm. About 700 people, adults and children, went for the day to Burgess Hill Pleasure Gardens by special train from Brighton Station. The children marched in orderly fashion – banners and flags flying – down Islingword Road, along Lewes Road to Trafalgar Street. There was great excitement on the train journey and we couldn't wait to get into the Pleasure Gardens and book a boat on the lake. After a lovely tea Mr Groves would ring the hand bell around the gardens for everyone to make their way to the station and return. The winter treat was held at the Mission and there was a prize-giving and a Magic Lantern show which consisted of animated animal pictures followed by slides of the summer treat.

Olive and Bernard Pelking

It was just 52 years ago (in 1999) that I first entered the doors of Islingword Road Mission, a place that was to become my second home. The Sunday School was large with over 200 pupils, ranging from under 5s in the side room to two Bible classes, the girls upstairs and the boys downstairs. On one Sunday a month there was church parade when the uniformed organisations and the rest of the Sunday School marched around the streets with a band and a banner with 'Islingword Road Mission' on it. This was 'a witness' and children would tag on from the streets.

Monday night was Girl Crusaders and we had a uniform of a white blouse with a green scarf, skirt and beret. I felt so proud wearing this as it made me equal with the other girls. Sometimes, during the winter evenings we met at 'Tindale' in 180 Freshfield Road, the home of Mr and Mrs Waldron, where we did handicrafts such as painting glasses for presents. It was lovely there with a nice coal fire and so homely. In the summer we sometimes went to the Racehill for stoolball or rounders. Every year we gave a display of marching, dumbbells, skipping and physical activities for parents and friends. I can also remember going with Miss Waite on a Saturday afternoon to entertain old people in Brighton General Hospital. Those early days were during wartime, when we experienced a lot of poverty; the Church supplied our physical as well as our spiritual needs.
Betty Gillett

St Joseph's church

St Joseph's church and school rooms in Milton Road were erected in 1869 for the Irish soldiers stationed in Brighton. After the opening of the permanent church in Elm Grove this building continued as a school and church hall, and has since been extended and reconstructed.

St Joseph's church and school rooms in Milton Road 1973

The churches and chapels of Hanover provided not only for the religious and educational needs of the community of the area, but also organised an annual summer outing which gave the children their only opportunity to travel further afield than their limited boundaries: often only the few streets in which they lived, shopped, went to school, had friends, later married and set up home for themselves.

THE BREWERY

Richard Tamplin, a mercer born in Dane Hill, moved to Brighton in 1811, and by 1820 he was trading as the Sussex County Bank of Castle Square with Creasy, Gregory and Company. In the same year he purchased a small brewery in Southwick from Nathaniel Hall, which was destroyed by fire shortly afterwards. In spite of suffering an uninsured loss of over £10,000, Tamplin appears to have taken temporary premises in Worthing before beginning to build a new brewery in Brighton. The plans were drawn up the following year by the architect Amon Henry Wilds, and the foundation stone was laid by Henry Pagden Tamplin, the brewer's eldest son.

The Phoenix brewery

It was this building, rising from the ashes, albeit on a different site, that became the 'Phoenix', soon to be the largest brewery in the county. By 1902 Tamplin's had occupied an area of 100,000 square feet bounded by Albion Street, Albion Hill, Newhaven and Southover Streets, employing 150 men. The Tamplins lived in a spacious house, at 1-3 Lennox Terrace, later Richmond Terrace, which became the company's offices. The counting house was a smaller red brick building at the entrance to the yard.

Richard Tamplin was partnered by his son Henry Pagden Tamplin, who after learning the trade, inherited the business on his father's death in 1849. Henry in turn was partnered by his eldest son William Cloves Tamplin, who inherited the business in 1867. So as to provide for his family of ten children, William transferred the business, valued at over £300,000, into a limited company in 1889, appointing himself as chairman. William commanded the First Volunteer Battalion of the Royal Sussex Regiment and his colonel built a drill hall in Church Street, Brighton at his own expense, which, with its fine doorway, can still be seen today. William died in 1893 leaving an estate worth over £200,000, but absolute control of the brewery passed out of the family.

The business expanded with the acquisition of the licensed houses of several smaller concerns. In 1892 the nearby Albion Brewery in Albion Street was purchased and the premises were retained as a wine, spirit and bottled beer store. In 1899 the number of outlets was increased with the acquisition of the licensed houses of the Catt family.

The next year saw the purchase of the 12 houses of the Brighton Brewery Company from R C Weekes, a brewery in Osborne Street, Hove. It was used as a store for a short time before being demolished. In the same year the business of the South Malling Brewery at Lewes was purchased from Bishop & Son. Eventually Tamplins owned 200, over two-thirds, of the licensed premises in the Brighton area, with a further 400 elsewhere.

Tamplins was taken over by Watneys in 1953, although the business continued unchanged for a while. The last brew was in 1973, and the brewery was demolished in 1980, although much of the bottling and storage building remained until recently, while the site was retained as a depot before operations were transferred to Lewes.

The last of the brewing buildings have now gone and the site is used for housing, although the red brick office and houses in Richmond Terrace, including numbers 1-3, have been retained. The name 'Phoenix' was revived recently on many of the public house signs, replacing the earlier 'Red Barrel', although there are still many old premises that state 'Tamplin's Entire' on the walls.

I attended St Luke's School until I was 14 and then went to work for Tamplin's Brewery. I worked from 5.30 am until 5.30 pm Monday to Friday and 5.30 am until 12 noon on Saturdays. I started each day by lighting the eight fires in the offices on the corner of Phoenix Place. The chemists who tested the beer worked there and I had to clean the grates and relay all the fires so that it was warm for them when they started work. At 8 am I had half-an-hour break in the back room to eat my sandwich. My main job then started in the tun room, where the big vats were. The vats were green after the beer had been emptied from them and had to be cleaned. I had to get into the tuns and clean them with bundles of steel wool and pumice powder. After two weeks my hands were like raw meat, but they gradually got used to it, and for this I received 10 shillings a week. They kept three pairs of horses and wagons at the back which were used to deliver the barrels to the pubs.
Gordon Harwood

Tamplins horses and wagons

*When I left school at 14 I went to work for Tamplin's Brewery. I worked in the tun room
and wore an apron and Wellington boots. I had to climb into the big tuns and with a wire
brush and a hose-pipe. I had to scrub all the pipes until they came up like brass. During
the war we were bombed and we all dived underneath the barrels for protection. There
was quite a lot of damage. I had to change to do war work when I was old enough and left
Tamplin's to work for Allen West, the engineering firm in Lewes Road.*
Vera Saunders

*I came to Tamplin's in 1962 from the parent company Watney Mann. Tamplin's was still
trading under its own name, and continued to do so until the end of the sixties. Tamplin's
had a bottling store at Cannon Place and Russell Street until the land was purchased for
Churchill Square. In 1964 a new bottling store was built on the Phoenix Brewery site and
operated until its closure in the early seventies. The end of 1973 was a sad time for
Tamplin's for it saw the end of brewing. The Phoenix Brewery became a distribution depot
with all products being bought in by trucker lorries mainly from Brick Lane, Isleworth,
and Mortlake Breweries. The company name changed again, this time to Watney's
Southern Ltd, and the early eighties saw what was to become the final change, to the
Phoenix Brewery Company.*

*From 1962 to 1975 I worked as an assistant transport manager. In the first two years I
would start work at 7 am and during the summer period it was not unusual to work until
8.30 pm. The draymen (lorry drivers and their mates) were on overtime payment, and a*

common practice then was for pub landlords to give the draymen a full lunch. The crews worked their rounds so they could arrive at the pub where they knew they could get the best food.

There were approximately 50 delivery vehicles then employing around 110 men as some vehicles had three men to handle deep and difficult pub cellars. Those were the years of hard physical work, but years with good camaraderie and a happy working atmosphere. A new system of payment was introduced for the draymen in 1965. This provided the delivery men with the opportunity to go home as soon as their day's work was completed; unsurprisingly the late summer working hours ceased.

The work of the draymen was then heavy, physical and thirst making, quenched in most cases with beer. It was not unusual for a drayman to consume up to 14 pints during the course of his work on a hot summer's day. They were also entitled to a two pint beer allowance each day in the brewery mess room. This ceased with the introduction of the breathalyser, improved mechanical handling and smaller containers. The days of hogsheads (54 gallon vessels) and barrels (36 gallons) had gone forever, to be replaced with metal containers of 22 and 11 gallons. I was offered redundancy and was pleased to accept it.

Michael Evans

I came to the Phoenix Brewery in 1952 as a professional brewer, becoming second brewer and eventually chief brewer. Each beer had its own recipe, and it was my responsibility to see that the ingredients were to hand and fed into the process at the right time. We used local barley from Lewes and hops from Kent, delivered to the brewery by road in hop pockets (sacks). We had about 50 men on the production side and had enormous tuns, large wooden copper lined vessels in which could made between 90 and 150 barrels of beer at a time. These had to be cleaned out with pumice stone after every process, which was very hard work. The brewery was closed in 1974, when it became a depot and I became depot manager. I retired in 1982. I look back at my time at the Phoenix with many fond memories.

Derek Nelmes

The Phoenix Brewery a major employer in the area in its heyday. It was sad to see the Malthouse disappear as it was such a beautiful flint building. At one time it was going to be used for artists' studios, but the cost of conversion was too high. Much of the site has now been used for student housing, which has again changed the character of this area. The red brick office is now used as a community centre, and the houses at 1 - 3 Richmond Terrace have been converted to flats.

PUBLIC HOUSES

Public houses in the Hanover area are as popular today as they were in the past. There was a beer house or inn on nearly every street corner. In 1867 there were five public houses in Southover Street, as there are today. In 1872 there were five inns and three beer retailers and by 1879 there were eight inns – the Greyhound and the Bricklayer's Arms being next door to one another.

In the 1870s the public house at the top of Southover Street, 'The Royal Exchange', was an inn where travellers could stay. It lost its name in the late 1990s, and is now known as 'The Pub with No Name'.

The Sir Charles Napier public house has many framed memorabilia collected by a former publican, Barry Hewland, on the walls.

The Charles Napier in Southampton Street annual ladies outing 1929

The Fox Inn (see back cover)
The Fox Inn was the first public house to be opened in Southover Street in c1845, with Peter Phillips as the landlord. The rest of the Southover Street was not developed until the 1850s and 60s. The Fox continued to be a public house until the 1920s when it was converted into houses. It is now a teashop, called the Tea Cosy, where good manners are strictly enforced.

My great-grandmother Mary was in service in a grand house just outside Brighton. She became pregnant by her employer, or his son, and a daughter Frances was born in 1850. Mary returned to Brighton and married John Page. The father of her daughter Frances, who had kept in contact with her, settled money on her and they bought the Fox Inn in Southover Street. Her daughter Frances, my grandmother, was brought up in The Fox, as well as in various cookshops and eating houses in the area. The original clock from The Fox Inn is still in the family.
Sonia Waterton

The Live and Let Live public house on the corner of Dinapore and Richmond Streets 1956. The barrier across Richmond Street was to stop horses slipping down the hill

I was the landlord of the Albion Pub from 1966-1992. The area was being developed when I took over. Richmond Heights was built by 1966 and Dinapore House was very run down. Chate's Farm was allotments and workshops, but by 1981 the Chate's Farm flats had been built. The area has changed, houses have been converted into flats and there are now more owner-occupiers and students. We tried to be a family pub when there were families in the small houses and it was very friendly, but that generation has gone and the new occupants have got their own way of life.
Dennis Alderson

In 1990 there were 235 public houses in the Borough of Brighton, one for every 600 inhabitants. Former public houses can still be recognised in many streets by their front doors set at an angle to the corner of the building.

Above: Sussex Street 1938 with a glimpse of the Lion & the Unicorn Inn, showing the barrier. The houses on the right were were demolished 1938/9

Below: the Beaufort public house c1910, at 175 Queens Park Road, when C S Ratcliffe was the publican, it is now the Beaufort Arms. The third house down the hill, with 'CHEMIST' painted on the wall, is still a chemist run by the O'Flinn's

Above: The Flowing Stream Public House 22/23 Newhaven Street closed 1953

Below: The Admiral Napier public house, Elm Grove 1934

WORLD WARS

Although the United Kingdom entered the war in August 1914, the summer season in Brighton continued in full swing. It was not until the first casualties arrived about a month later that the reality of the conflict hit the inhabitants,

The War later affected most people who lived in the close-knit community of Hanover. Father William Carey was the incumbent of the Church of the Annunciation during the War and kept up a correspondence with members of the congregation who were involved in combat.

France 1915 – George Strong, 1st Sussex Battery

"How is everybody at the dear old Annunciation? I hope you get good congregations at Mass on Sundays, although I expect you get fewer men. We don't go to church now, as we are not allowed near the church; but we generally have a service in our canteen. Jack sent me the June Parish magazine. I hear all the club chaps have joined the Army, and I should think the dear old Annunciation has contributed to the Motherland… Have you a Role of Honour? Let me know how many are on it . . . I always think of the little church on the hill, and shall be very glad when the war is over and I can get back to those I love and all my [many] dear friends."

Sapper Reg Hilder – wrote from Eastbourne

"Well, I started soldiering properly now. There's rifle drill, trench digging, route marching with full kit, field geometry, hurdle-making, etc. It's quite a puzzle trying to get your kit together. Glad to say my arm is better now after inoculation, but each day brings the second dose nearer. I've met T Pelling up here as well as one or two other Annunciationites. It makes me feel more at home when we are all together. Tomorrow we get church parade at 9 am; it's a fine sight to see all the fellows and the band marching along to the church. I might say that we've got plenty of aeroplanes over here and an airship; these are flying from any time after 6 am."

October 1915 – Jack Strong RAF France

"Just a line to thank you for the crucifixes. I have given them both away, and the chaps who received them, wish to thank you . . . for them . . . could you send me a song book to help us keep merry? I have got a wooden crucifix which I found in a village destroyed by the Germans, which I will send home to you at the first opportunity."

1916 – Jack Strong On Her Majesty's Service

"There were some of the Royal Sussex Regiment in the village and I ran across one of the old Annunciation boys… my old chum Percy Nicholls. He was billeted in a village . . . close to where I am lodging in a railway tunnel, which are draughty places to live in. I have been in France over a year and consider myself to be an old soldier. I hear brother Reggie has had a turn in the trenches… I am on duty until 5am so I can write some letters. We have a little dog which we keep as a mascot and have some fine sport with him as he is a fine rat catcher. I heard from George recently who hopes to complete his tour round the world soon! We have a stream which runs close by so we can have a bathe, a luxury for us."

Annunciation Sunday School Recruiting March – 7 November 1915
Reverend Basil Shelley, assistant priest

We did not touch the borders of the Parish. Our route lay through Hanover Terrace along Howard Road to Elm Grove and back again via Hampden Road, Islingword, Ewart and Jackson Streets and so on into church.

It was clear from the start that if we did nothing else we would rouse the Parish. Boys hovered like bees around the band. People stood and watched us in the street; while some followed. Doors and windows opened and men were roused from the Sunday siesta to see us go by. Women, children and babies in arms were among the spectators. At the corner of the 'Island' in Islingword Road we called a halt and after a recruiting speech and a hymn, we marched on again along Islingword Street. Back in church we had a short service and sifted out the recruits and took their names and addresses. There were 52 in all.

However, when Sunday came, not all our recruits arrived; others, not reckoned with, put in an appearance. We had at least 40 children, which was not bad.

The effect of the First World War on Hanover

It was not until the first casualties started to arrive in Brighton in September 1914 that the reality of the conflict hit the inhabitants of the town. The Poor Law Institution in Elm Grove, now Brighton General Hospital, was one of several major Brighton buildings given to the military for use as hospitals.

Second World War . . .

Albion Hill and its surrounding area was hit by two heavy calibre bombs. One landed at the junction of Albion Hill and Ashton Street, demolishing a butcher's shop and killing the owner William Chubb. Nellie Vincent of 13 Albion Hill, aged 57, was pulled from the wreckage alive but died from her wounds in hospital. Cambridge and Ashton Streets were badly hit by bombs. Nearly 30 houses were so badly damaged that they had to be demolished. The bombs caused minor damage to houses in a quarter of a mile radius and the streets were littered with glass.

The raid started just after 3.30 pm without warning, although the bomber had been seen for several minutes and was easily distinguishable as a German raider. The second bomb landed in a garden which wrecked houses in Cambridge and Dinapore Streets. An oil bomb fell close by and exploded, wrecking a house at the junction of Cambridge Street and Albion Hill; the houses on the opposite side of the road were covered in crude oil. Several streets had to be evacuated including the Phoenix Brewery, for which, it is thought, the bombs were meant. Most of the injured were children who had not long been out of school and were playing in the streets.

In all 33 houses were demolished as well as the Sir John Falstaff pub at 137 Albion Hill. Many families were sheltered at Congress Hall overnight, and they returned to salvage what belongings they could from the wreckage the following day; German fighters appeared overhead and machine-gunned them. Terrified, they lay in the gutter and covered their heads with their hands.

During the war years, what is the now the Community Centre was taken over by the Royal Electrical and Mechanical Engineers. I was engaged to a soldier training there. Enemy air raiders tried many times to set light to Tamplin's Brewery. Bombs hit the end of Lewes Street, demolished a paper shop and a huge piece of masonry crashed through our shop window. Luckily no one in our shop was hurt.
Eve King

On the day in 1940 the bomb hit my aunt's shop I was the only girl working at Bleco's in St Martin's Place, making small parts for bombs. I had been there about three months and we were on the roof eating our sandwiches when we heard a plane overhead making a funny noise. We looked up in bright sunlight and Len Anscombe said, "It's alright, it's one of ours", and we could see the red, white and blue under the wings. It was flying north along Lewes Road, then it suddenly returned and we saw the swastikas on the wings, heard a terrible bang and saw clouds of smoke. A bomb had hit the Lewes Road Inn at the bottom of Franklin Road and Peter Williams, the manager, was killed. We went back into work and I was called to see the boss and given sweet tea. I was worried because I thought I'd done something wrong, but they told me that my aunt's shop had received a direct hit. They sent me home in the firm's lorry.

51

We managed to get round by Phoenix Place, but when we got to the bottom of the hill it was devastated. I remember going up to the shop and I started screaming because I knew our house was next door. A Salvation Army lass came over and gave me some tea in a jam jar and they told me that my mother, sister, aunt and cousin had been taken to hospital. My father arrived, having seen the smoke of the bomb from the wall at Brighton Station and thought it seemed near our home, which was badly damaged. Johnny Knight lived next door, and I could hear a boy crying in the rubble. The men said they'd looked there but I said that I recognised his voice as he was Scottish. They started digging and I spotted his hand. They got him out, but his legs were badly smashed. If I see him he always says, "You saved my life". We were all taken to the Citadel by The Level where we were given blankets and hot cocoa and thick bread from Hobden's, the baker in London Road.

Seven members of my family were in Bristol ward at the Sussex County Hospital. While they were there I went out dancing at Sherry's with a friend called Ruby Grinyer and on the way home there was an air raid. We rushed into what we thought was an empty house, but beyond the front door was a drop and I fell and injured my leg. I ended up in a camp bed on Bristol ward between my mother and grandmother.

Albion Hill bombed in 1940, one of the worst hit areas in the town

52

The Ebenezer Chapel in Richmond Street (photograph page 38), the Duke of Cambridge and the Lennox Arms pubs were bombed. I was asked to be an Air Raid Warden but I'd only been training for four weeks when we had a scare and had to go to the shelter between Albion Hill and Southover Street. The cement was still wet when we reached it, but they had a 'phone and tea and a bucket behind the door in case we needed it. Albion Street was bombed in the war and all the little cobbled cottages went and they rebuilt the area with houses and flats.
Jackie Griffiths

The Newhaven Street area was bombed on my son Brian's seventh birthday. I was lying on my bed when my husband came in and said that Lewes Street and Dinapore Street had been bombed. Brian was at Richmond Street School and I ran over to my friend Win's house and shouted, "There's a bomb down the bottom of our street and the kids are in school". I only had slippers on but I ran all the way down the street to the school and saw a little girl lying on the step outside the Falstaff Pub in Albion Hill. Miss Coombs the headmistress met us and said, "The children are alright". So I went home and thought I'd better get my Brian's party ready.

Mrs Twell from Dinapore Street, who had six children, was blinded, Mr Flood the butcher was killed. They came round and said we'd have to get out of our houses because a time bomb had been dropped on the brewery. I said, "I'm not going, if it goes up I'll go too". The next day my husband went for a drink and he rushed back and said, "Get down here quick, they're just about to let the time bomb off". I jumped down the stairs top to bottom.
Kathleen Lilley

Bombs affected the Chates Farm area badly. There was a butcher's shop that was absolutely flattened. My Uncle Bill worked at the shop but he was on an errand when the bomb dropped. Uncle Bill lived in Lewes Street and when he returned home he found his own house was blown to pieces and his daughter had been blown across the room out of her chair, but she survived. His family moved in with my grandparents in Grove Street and they were rehoused in Lincoln Street.
Roy Wilkinson

My stepfather ran a grocery shop at 32 Richmond Buildings. It was my job to cut out all the coupons, count them and send them to the Ministry of Food. I put my age up by a year so that I could join the Home Guard and I fire-watched at the Royal Alexandra Hospital.
John Rackham

We lived at 58 Southampton Street, there were seven boys and four girls in the family. When the Second World War broke out all the boys enlisted, one in the Air Force and six in the Army. The Herald took our picture in the back yard, also of the Perrin family opposite who had eight sons who enlisted. We were lucky, all seven of us returned from the war.
Frank Edwards

The effect of the Second World War on Hanover

The Second World War had a much greater effect on Brighton than the First World War. Shelters were dug in parks and playgrounds. Albion Hill was one of the most seriously bombed areas in the town. Brighton greeted Victory in Europe Day, 8 May 1945, with great celebrations and many street parties. Further celebrations were held on Victory in Japan Day, 15 August 1945.

Victory celebration party in Cambridge Street

SCHOOLS

Education during the nineteenth century was mainly confined to the children of the wealthy, with poor children relying on a haphazard arrangement of Dame Schools, Sunday Schools and eventually Church Schools for their education.

As the population from Carlton Hill spilled into Hanover the demand for school places increased, and the churches were quick to respond. The Belgrave Street Chapel School opened in 1863, was swiftly followed by St Mary's Boys' School at the Church of the Annunciation in 1864. St Joseph's School in Milton Road opened in 1874 to cater for the increase in Catholic families in the town.

The Education Act of 1870 enabled Board Schools to be set up in districts where there were insufficient schools to cater for the number of children. During the next 30 years Thomas Simpson designed many of the Board Schools which still remain in use in Brighton today and make such notable punctuation marks in the townscape of the city.

Belgrave Street School
Belgrave Street School opened in 1863 with a schoolroom, used as an Infants' School and opened for public worship in the same year. The Congregational Church was active in poorer areas of the town and had identified a need for a school in Hanover. Brighton School Board took control as soon as it was founded, and rooms at the Belgrave Street Chapel continued to be used as a small school until 1924, when it was closed and the children dispersed amongst other schools. The building later became an annexe to the University of Brighton, and has now being converted into housing and is now called Billam Terrace.

St Mary's Boys' School
St Mary's Boys' School (late School of the Annunuciation) was opened in 1865 by the Reverend A D Wagner with 21 boys, and moved to Southover Street in 1872. The letters 'SM' can still be seen carved over the front entrance. It was known as St Paul's School when the Annunciation was served by curates from St Paul's church. It became the Annunciation School in about 1900, the Corporation's Handicraft School in 1924, the Southover Street Canteen – or soup kitchen as it was known in the 1930s, an education supply store after the war and is now the Hanover Community Centre.

St Joseph's Roman Catholic School

St Joseph's Roman Catholic School, a small church school, was opened in Milton Road in 1879 in premises built as a church to cater for the Irish Catholic soldiers who were stationed in Brighton.

The premises were small and the largest room was divided into four classrooms. As early as 1908 the Inspector was condemning the premises as being inadequate for the teaching of children, but Brighton Council was not prepared to pay for a new building. The school catered for children aged between 5 -14, but later in the century if the boys passed the scholarship examination at 11, they could go to the Xaverian College.

The band of St Joseph's school 1938

The head of St Joseph's was a Miss Mattimore and her sister was the senior teacher; Miss Chapel ran the infants' department in a classroom on its own. Other classes were taught together, with two rows of desks for one class and and two for the other, with one teacher for both. One group would be taught whilst the other group got on with work and then the arrangement was reversed for the next lesson. The boys had to walk to Belgrave Street School to do carpentry, the girls walked to Montpelier Road for cookery classes, and both groups had to walk to and from the Wild Park for their physical education lessons.

The hours were 9 am - 12 noon and 2 - 4 pm with a two hour break for lunch. There were no school dinners so we all had to go home. The bell was rung to let us know when school was starting and ending. We had a small bottle of milk every day and when it was cold in winter, a monitor would bring it in and put the crate near the fire to warm it up. Nurses, who we called 'Nitty Nora', came to inspect our hair and if you were found to have nits you had to stand in the playground until your mother came to collect you. Once a year a doctor came to measure and weigh you.

There wasn't very much space for the children at playtime and the girls went into the small back garden whilst the boys played in Milton Road, there was not much traffic in the 1930s. There was a pub called the Elm Grove Tavern on the other corner of Milton Road and Elm Grove and the publican didn't like the boys playing in the road as he feared his windows would get broken. Eventually the school bought the house next door and we were able to use that garden as well.
Patrick Cheeseman and Margaret Miller

It was not until 1956 that the Church was able to fund a new school in Hollingdean, where St Joseph's remains to this day.

Hanover Board School, Hanover Terrace
The Brighton & Preston Board School purchased land in Coleman Street and Hanover Terrace between 1872 and 1901 to build Hanover Terrace Board School. This area was described as lying in Islingword Furlong in Hilly Laine.

The school was opened in 1873. When the schools were reorganised in 1928, Hanover Terrace School became a Junior Mixed and Senior Boys' School only, while pupils of the Senior Girls' and Infants' department, which closed in 1932, moved to other local schools.

During the Second World War numbers dropped dramatically and the school was threatened with closure. It closed after the war and was used by the Secondary Technical School. Planning permission was granted in 1999 to replace the building with houses.

I started at Hanover Terrace School when I was five. We didn't have bottles of milk or school dinners so we went home for dinner. The girl next to me was quite well off as she always had fruit to eat. The only time we had apples was when we went scrumping along the lane at the bottom of Southover Street where the trees hung over the wall.

I spent very little time in school as my mother was always ill and confined to bed so my father would say "You can't go to school today", because there was always a baby in the house, but the boys didn't have to look after babies. I don't think I ever did a full week at school and I grew to loathe it because I was away so much I couldn't catch up. I used to think "Why should I learn about history when there are children to look after". I can remember coming out of my house in Hanover Terrace and bending low in front of our little wall, and looking up and down the street before I came out to see if the School Board Man was about. I dodged him most of the time but he caught me once. If my father had written a note it would have been alright. I used to get my knuckles rapped with a ruler because I was away so much, so I resented the school and authority.

Before I went to school I used to go to a fruiterer, Measors, at 114 Islingword Road, as they also sold coal. I used to get 28lb bag of coal on a trolley and wheel it down Southover Street so that we'd have coal for the day. I then lugged this coal sack into the house and

Pupils at Hanover Terrace Board School in Hanover Terrace c1890

Sampler worked by Emily Simms, pupil at Hanover Terrace Board School c1875

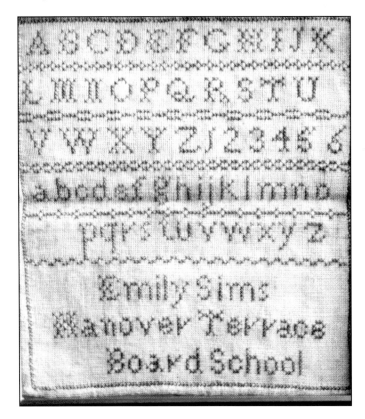

put it into the cupboard in the passage and took the trolley back. This particular day I arrived at school with filthy hands and I was sitting in the front of the class when the headmistress came in. She said, 'How dare you come to school with such filthy hands, go and wash them immediately". The children giggled when I returned to class. Miss Long, who was teaching us, said, "How many children helped your mothers this morning? You all laughed at Dorothy Page, but she is up early to fetch coal for her mother."

We had to have plimsolls for sport as we normally wore heavy boots, but I hadn't any. We all said we forgotten them, and for that we would get a whack across the hand.
Dorothy Farrell

I passed the scholarship for Varndean but my parents couldn't afford to send me there, as we had to pay for our own paper, pencils and uniform and my father had retired from his railway job.
Jackie Griffiths

Richmond Street Board School
Richmond Street Board School was opened in 1873 and with Hanover Terrace School served a large, mainly poor catchment area. The school ran from Richmond Street to Sussex Street fronting Claremont Row. It was an imposing building which stretched along the whole street with the Girls School at the Richmond Street end and the Boys School at the Sussex Street end. The playgrounds separated the two schools and overlooked the houses in Ivory Place.

Hanover Terrace School 1928

When the school was amalgamated with Circus Street School in 1927, they were known as the Sussex Street Schools. In 1959 the area came under a Compulsory Purchase Order and Richmond Street was demolished. The Circus Street School building survived and still used by the University of Brighton, though there are now plans to demolish it as part of the plan for the Circus Street area.

Brighton Education Committee School Building Annual Report 31.3.1911:
Arrangements are to be made for the feeding of necessitous school children at Richmond Street, Park Street and Elm Grove in the winter and at Richmond Street in the summer.

1912: Breakfast is to be provided for poor children during the Christmas and Easter holidays which will consist of hot milk and buns.

HMI Report Sussex Street Schools – January 1925: The social conditions of the neighbourhood greatly influence the curriculum and aims of teaching at this school. A large share of the teachers' efforts must necessarily be given to the general training of the girls, arousing healthy ambitions, directing effort and developing self-control, while all suffer from restricted opportunity and outlook. Much has been done to secure cleanliness and to encourage self-respect. The retarded need more specialised treatment than can be given in an ordinary elementary school.

HMI Report Sussex Street Schools 1927: Boys generally behave well and showed willingness during the inspection. Standard 10 . . . too readily to become playful.

HMI Report Sussex Street School Junior Mixed 1930: Two classes have over 50 pupils. Training in good social habits.

HMI Report Sussex Street Schools Infants 1934:
Since this school is situated in a district where the mothers need all the help they can be given them, a Nursery class was formed in October 1930 with 17 children aged 3 years which has now increased to 37 children. There is also a transition class of 40 four year olds. They enjoy free activity and sleep and are taught good habits, cleanliness, self-help, obedience and good temper in play.

I went to Richmond Street Infants' School which was just opposite our shop, so I didn't have to go far. Every afternoon we would be put on our little beds for a sleep. There was an old sink with goldfish in it which I enjoyed looking at. Of course the toilets were outside. Later I transferred to Circus Street School but had to be transferred again when St John's closed down.
Connie Dowds

We would come down Richmond Street and climb over the wall of the Girls' School to take a short cut through their playground to the Boys' School. As Richmond Street was a steep hill you could look through the railings into the bedrooms of a row of small cottages in Ivory Place below. Mothers would often pass food through the railings to their children in the playground.

Charles Moore

Finsbury Road Board School

Finsbury Road Board School was opened in 1881, in 1903 the pupils were transferred to the new St Luke's School while alterations were made. The school reopened in 1904 and as Bentham Road Infants' School had closed, the children were transferred to Finsbury Road. It became an Infants' and Junior Mixed School from 1928, the senior pupils being transferred to other schools. The Infants' School closed in 1955 and the Junior Mixed School in 1956. The premises were used by St Luke's School and then became an annexe to Brighton Polytechnic, later the University of Brighton. In 1999 the University applied for planning permission to demolish the school and replace it with housing. The building was subsequently listed as of architectural and historical interest and the University applied for permission to convert it to flats.

Finsbury Road Board School

HMI Report Febuary 1908:

The influence of the school is a healthy one and the girls are carefully trained in the right habits, but in some classes might be rather more alert and ready in geography. The curriculum includes reading, recitation, composition, arithmetic, history and geography. The Infants are carefully trained in habits of neatness and of cheerful obedience. This was practically a new school three years ago and was not very fortunate in the boys who were drafted into it on its reopening.

61

HMI Report Junior Mixed 1930

The largest class was 59 pupils as there was a bulge of 10-year olds. Too much needlework is attempted in the top classes.

I went to Finsbury Road, but had cooking lessons at Elm Grove School. My father was sometimes out of work and I would receive tickets for food and have free school meals at Elm Grove.

Harriett Waldron

Plaque on Finsbury Road school

My grandfather Monk used to work for Carter Patterson Carriers delivering wines, spirits, and gas and paraffin stoves from the station. He had a horse drawn cart with a 'dickie seat'. The horse was stabled in the station yard and if he had deliveries in the Finsbury Road area at 4.30 pm he would reach across with his whip to tap at the classroom window and take out his watch to show the teacher the time. Miss Hills, the teacher, used to say "Your granddaughter has two minutes to go" and he would say "Right, I'll come and fetch her then", at which point I would be allowed to leave. I would sit on the back of the cart with my legs dangling down and get a lift home.

Jackie Griffiths

I was born in Montreal Road in 1926 and lived there until 1948. I attended Finsbury Road School from the age of four. The school was divided into Infants, Junior Mixed and Senior Girls. Mr Tierney, the caretaker, lived in a house next to the boys' entrance at 59 Southampton Street which had a door from his garden leading to the playground. Needless to say we had outside toilets.

There were quite a lot of poor children from large families, especially in Southampton Street, and sometimes they had very little in the way of clothes and shoes.

Scholarship examinations were taken at aged 10 or 11 over two days at Park Street School. We were given a pen and ruler to take with us and told if we lost them we would have to pay for them. If you passed the examination you could go to the Intermediate School in York Place and if you passed with exceptionally high marks you took another examination to go to Varndean School.

Cookery classes were held at Sussex Street School and later at Pelham Street School. Netball, hockey, etc, were played at Moulsecoomb playing fields just past the Preston Barracks. We walked there in a crocodile style and those lucky enough to have a penny could catch the tram home.

In 1939 there were only 100 girls in the school and it was decided to close it and I finished my last three terms at Elm Grove, some of it part time, as by now the evacuees were arriving from London and the school was shared.
E Campbell

I attended Finsbury Road School until I was 14. The school bell rang when school was about to start but on the way there I would be sent to a shop in Islingword Road, where they would accept bets, illegal then. My dad would write down a bet and say "As you run round the corner just call in with this." I didn't like doing this and would insist that it would make me late for school, but he would say, "No you won't, just run". I'd put my head round the door and say "Dad said…". I would leave the bet and run off to school as the bell was ringing
Vera Saunders

Yours affectionately
A Pedish
First Head Mistress
of
Elm Grove School
1893 to 1923

Head of Elm Grove School 1895-1923

Elm Grove Board School

Elm Grove Board School opened in 1893 when over 300 children from Bentham Road Infants' School were transferred, but by the end of the summer term the school role had risen to 800, including 438 infants. From 1928 the site was occupied by Senior Girls, Junior Mixed and Infants; the Senior Boys being dispersed to other schools. In spite of a fear in the 1980s that the school might be closed when the numbers fell, Elm Grove still remains as a primary school.

HMI Report 1904:

Boys are carefully taught, discipline excellent, singing extremely well taught, drawing good. Girls – good methods are adopted in instruction and thoroughly satisfactory results are consequently obtained. Jessie Bevis employed as a monitress in the Infant Department at two shillings a week.

HMI Report 1905

Girls – The school is overfull and there are not sufficient desks for all the children.

HMI Report 1913

Boys – The syllabus in history, geography and science is above the heads of the boys. The teachers have become lecturers, boys listeners. French has been withdrawn from the timetable and science much reduced.

Girls – High estimate on manners and behaviour but considerable weakness on the intellectual side. Attainments of the girls are far too much on the surface and rest upon no solid foundation.

HMI Report 1921

Boys – Industrious and respond readily. Only 20 of the 186 eligible boys at present attend the Handicraft Centre.

Girls – Pleasant and happy conditions but disappointed that none of the girls reached the Ex VIIth Standard. English well done, arithmetic weaker.

Elm Grove school

Bentham Road School

Bentham Road School opened in 1896 in a church building which consisted of one large hall with three classrooms and the usual outbuildings. Twenty-nine children were admitted during the first week, aged between three and four years, none of whom knew the alphabet. On 19 June ten more children had been admitted but all were backward. The elder children were working with them to teach them the alphabet and short words.

In 1896 there were many cases of whooping cough and there were some absences when the weather was bad, but the intake had increased to 71. Some children were transferred to Elm Grove as the numbers grew, but the Inspector's Report in 1898 stated that: "These are inconvenient premises and the Board will, I trust, erect suitable permanent buildings as speedily as are practicable. Discipline is excellent."

In 1901 there was a great deal of sickness amongst the children, with such large classes the infections spread quickly. When the school reopened after the summer holidays a notice was received from the Medical Officer of Health to exclude all children from Islingword and Southampton Streets because of an epidemic of diphtheria.

In 1902 sixty children went from the school to have boots fitted, a present from the 'New Years Dinner & Boot Fund' Committee. The Inspector still complained about the unsuitable premises, but to no avail. In 1904 a strongly worded report was sent to the School Board:

> "It behoves the Education Authority of the Borough to remove young children
> speedily from unsuitable, unhygienic premises."

Bentham Road School was finally closed in 1904 with children transferred to Elm Grove and Finsbury Road Schools.

In 1906 the Education (Provision of Meals) Act was brought in and the Education Committee provided meals in the areas where they felt it was necessary.

The state system of school medical inspections began as a result of the Education (Administrative Provision) Act 1907. This enabled medical inspections of children immediately before, at the time of, or as soon as possible after, admission to the school. Attendance on the days of the medical inspections was found to be very low.

Under the Employment of Children Act 1910, the Inspectors in Brighton found that 1,683 boys and 265 girls were illegally employed out of school hours. The worst schools included: Richmond Street Girls: 52; Finsbury Road Girls: 44; Hanover Terrace Boys: 108; and Girls: 10. Jobs they were employed in included working in barbers' shops and licensed houses. Seventy-one boys and eight girls worked on milk or paper rounds and 160 boys worked as errand boys. Twenty boys and one girl were employed after 9 pm and many girls under 10 found employment minding a baby or running errands, often unpaid.

LAUNDRIES

The area of Hanover, like many other poorer areas, saw numerous hand laundries set up in small terrace houses to enable women to supplement the often meagre wages of the men. Many jobs, such as building, declined in winter and women often had to find ways to keep the family fed and clothed. Laundry work was dominated by married and widowed women, which could be adapted to fit in with domestic responsibilities and was unusual in that it could be carried out over a lifetime.

In the 1851 census Hanover Street had 68 households and 20 women, including nine widows, involved in laundry work. Hanover Terrace had 57 households, including 42 laundresses, four of whom are quoted employing other women, with five ironers. Contemporary maps show that there were laundry fields on the slopes behind Hanover Street, and this facility combined with the opportunities for obtaining work from the middle class developments of Hanover and Park Crescents would have made the area attractive to women who needed to make a living.

Some of the hand laundries developed into larger concerns, for example the Cobden Road Hand Laundry, which employed about six women from the area, and Gochers in Islingword Road which was mechanised and still remains in business today, though it is no longer in Hanover.

My maternal grandmother, Ann Shepherd aged 12, was sent to Brighton from Barcombe Mills to work at her aunt's laundry at 29 Henry Street. She married Arthur Berry in 1891, he was a jolly man who liked a drink and the races, and always dressed in a brown suit and bowler hat. He was a general labourer, but my grandmother, who was trained in laundry work, decided to run a laundry from her home to supplement their income. They moved to Sutherland Road in 1891 and later to 4 Toronto Terrace, where a laundry called the Imperial Laundry had already been established by a Mrs Scarterfield. My mother's brothers were all a dab hand at ironing and Arthur had a handcart with which he collected and delivered the laundry.

Unfortunately Arthur died in 1915 aged 45, leaving my grandmother to bring up the family with the proceeds from the laundry. She employed several women, and was very upset when the law changed and she had to pay women's insurance stamps. After the war she married the man next door who was a gardener. She sold the laundry in 1926/7.
Jennifer Besbrode

There were times when my father was out of work and we relied on my mother's cleaning job at the hospital in Elm Grove, and the nurses' washing she brought home. She would scrub all evening. There was a long stool in the scullery and in the corner a copper and two big wooden tubs. Dad made her a long ironing board and she put the big black iron in the grate to heat up.

Sometimes I would be sent to the jug and bottle department at the Sir Charles Napier pub in Southover Street to buy a drink for my grandmother. I could see women in the pub wearing caps and rough aprons, who I thought looked rather rough, I think they worked in the laundries in Finsbury Road opposite the 'bad girls' home'.

Harriett Waldron

I was born at 13 Arnold Street, the youngest of four girls. I attended Elm Grove School and left when I was 14. The school didn't help me get a job, but it was important that we started work as soon as possible. My mother went to Mrs Eves who ran a small hand laundry at 2 Arnold Street and asked if she had any vacancies. I left school on the Friday and started with Mrs Eves on the Monday, ironing handkerchiefs all day with a big metal iron that you heated on a stove. I worked from 8 am – 6 pm for five shillings a week and stuck it for a year. One of my older sisters worked at a laundry, she put in a word for me and I started with her for 25 shillings a week.

Betty Ticehurst

I left St John's School in Carlton Hill in the early 1930s aged 14 and went to work in the Model Laundry in Brading Road run by a Mr Farlington. I went to this laundry as women neighbours of ours in William Street worked there. I received 7s/6d a week for working 8am – 8 pm Monday and Tuesday when all the laundry came in and needed sorting for washing, and 8 am – 6 pm for the other three days – sorting, marking, racking, pressing, folding and using the hydro – a drier that spun the washing. The blankets would be hung out or put in drying rooms. Quite a lot of people in the street worked at the laundry.

Advertisement from a Street Directory

THE QUEEN'S PARK

LAUNDRY & CLEANING WORKS

(Established 28 Years),

31, TORONTO TERRACE, QUEEN'S PARK, BRIGHTON.

———:o:———

Proprietor—MR. HENRY CURCHOD.

Manageress Laundry Department—MRS. HENRY CURCHOD.

———:o:———

There were a lot of hand workers who starched collars and polished the machines. At Gochers laundry we had presses, one was the shape of a man's leg that we pulled the men's woollen socks over to keep their shape. We sent some of the ironing out to women in their own homes. It was mostly girls who worked in the laundry, except for a couple of maintenance men who turned down the steam from the calender when it got too hot. We used the calender – like a mangle – for the big sheets. Two people stood in front feeding in the sheets and two stood behind to collect them.

We wore white starched overalls and it was terribly hot when all the machines were working, although we always had the windows open and the fans going. On Thursdays everything would go to the packing room where it would be sorted into pigeonholes using the laundry mark, ticked off in the customers' book and tied into a brown paper parcel for delivery by van.

The staff rest room was underground and very dark and I didn't like to sit down there during my lunch hour. There was always a good atmosphere in the laundry with the other girls and we sometimes had a sing-song. I belonged to the 'perm club' where we contributed 6d a week and every week we had a draw to see who would get the 8s/6d for their perm.

Later I went to work at Cobden Road Hand Laundry. This wasn't as mechanised as Gochers but I really liked it and the owner was a lovely person. Miss Winder did the handwashing – the woollens, silks and delicates, and they were hung out to dry in the garden or, if the weather was bad, they would be put on lines around a coke boiler to dry. Each of us had two hand irons on the go at one time, one would be round the coal fires stove heating up while the other was in use. It wasn't until later that gas irons were used.

I left the laundry when I married, I think they were sorry to see me go.
Roseann West

The Quebec Laundry was in Quebec Street where there was always a lovely fresh soapy smell; all the sheets were hung out to dry along the back of the gardens of Quebec Street and Montreal Road. I don't know what happened if it rained, but at the end of the week the clean sheets were delivered back to their owners, starched and dazzling white, neatly tied in brown paper parcels
June Marshall..

When my husband was made redundant as a British Rail driver we had to find another way of bringing in the income. I heard from a school friend that her grandmother, Mrs Bellchamber, who had been at school with my grandfather, wanted to retire from the laundry in Cobden Road opposite the Cobden Arms, so we bought her business.

It wasn't a trade that you liked, but you had to make a living and we stayed there for 28 years. It was called the 'Cobden House Hand Laundry', but we dropped the 'Hand' when we had our first washing machine. There were other laundries in the street which looked like private houses. There was a roller shuttered entrance at the side of ours which led to a large piece of level land with apple and pear trees, which was used for drying blankets and other washing.

We had eight staff, four washers and four ironers. The ironers were on the ground floor with the washing area behind. The ironers worked from Tuesday to Friday from 8am – 4.30 pm with an hour for lunch. The packers were on the first floor where they had racks where the clothes were sorted. On Friday morning the clothes would be collected from the rack, checked against the laundry books and packed into neat brown paper parcels for delivery on Saturday.

There was no machinery at first, but we gradually mechanised with roller machines and a 'hydro' for drying and electric irons. Originally we had a big iron stove with four tiers which would heat up 100 irons. We were governed by the 'Factory Act', so we had inspectors to look at our machines. We had ironing machines for handkerchiefs, pillow cases and towels and revolving lathes overhead for the washing machines. All the small laundries helped each other, if our driver was out another would help.

On Mondays my husband collected the dirty laundry with laundry marks in red cotton. We took whites, cottons, woollens and silks. The sheets, pillow cases and towels would all go into the washing machine. If we had too much to cope with we would ask another laundry to help, we never turned work away. The Tivoli Laundry in Crescent Road would take up to 100 sheets and Gochers sometimes helped too. Miss Tarner, of Tarner Nursery fame, was among our customers, as was Mrs Allen [the wife of the director of the Allen West factory in Lewes Road] who lived at The Drive in Hove. We had four rounds in Brighton.

We had a loyal staff, mainly elderly women, all except the driver who was always a man. It was hard work and there was a lot of steam, especially when the copper was boiling and the ironers got steam from the washroom because it was at the same level.

We lived in the flat on the second floor.
Laundry owner

By the 1950s everything changed with the introduction of launderettes, then later washing machines in individual homes, though there are still a scattering of launderettes.

STREET LIFE

Most of the densely populated district had become known as Hanover from about 1880. It typically consisted of small terraces with angular window bays. Since being designated a 'general improvement area' in 1969 - 1976, Hanover has become a more attractive residential district, and has escaped the massive redevelopment of the adjacent Albion Hill.

Few people knew about Chates Farm hidden in the triangle of Albion Hill, Richmond Street and Liverpool Street. It was approached by a narrow lane from 116 Albion Hill.

Edward Tilbury Esq owned 27 perches of land which was occupied by Obidiah Dray in 1851. He had a cowstall, stable, yard and eight cows. It later became Chate's Farm which was established in the 1860s, the cows were grazed on land across Albion Hill where Grove Street is now. This street was not built until 1894, many years later than the neighbouring streets. The cows were then taken to graze on Tarner's land off Richmond Street, which in turn was built on in 1930. The Chate family lived in 34 Richmond Street with stables and cow stalls adjoining.

Delivery of milk ceased during the First World War but customers were still served at the premises until about 1934.

Opposite: Thornsdale flats being built in 1960 taken from Highleigh

Below: Richmond Farm dairy at Chate's Farm 1934

Liverpool Street looking east to Chate's Farm with Albion Hill on the left 1963

Chate's Farm was built on Tarner's land and the farmers were all tenant farmers, as were the Chate family, who were dairy farmers who also sold eggs and rhubarb. Before the first World War, George Chate, had a milk business in Hamilton Road. He had to get rid of it in the war as he was called up, but after the war he bought a shop in Windmill Terrace selling milk, eggs, butter and cheese. George sold his business when the Co-op came into the area to deliver milk.

Our parents became tenants of the Chates in the 1930s. When we moved into the farm house as children, the farm buildings were being used as workshops and garages and were surrounded by the farm which backed onto Liverpool Street. Milk was still being sold, served from the 'Can House', reached by a little path along which people would come with their jugs. We now use this building for our washing.

Mr Chate retired from work at the age of 40 to look after his ill wife. He moved with his wife and daughter into a bungalow which he built in the garden (see the photograph above). It was bought by the Council after their death. We would have liked to move in to it, but the Council decided to put in a family with a great many children. When they left it was so badly damaged it had to be demolished.

We could sit at the side of the house in the evenings and look across Brighton; it was a marvellous view. All that changed in the 1960s when they demolished much of the area and built an enormous block of flats which blocked our view.

The Tarners sold their land bit by bit. A planning application was submitted to build a block of flats, now called 'Chate's Farm Court', where the old farm buildings were. We objected to the original scheme because the spur of the flats would have been right in front of us. Fortunately they changed the plan so we still have some of our view left. When they came to build the flats the slight camber on the farm land made a big drop into Liverpool Street and to save putting a lift in the flats they built them on two levels with access from both sides.

Ralph and Daphne Howard

50 Southampton Street Abstract of Title 15th June 1869, later the site of the pickle factory

"A conveyance between Thomas Wisden of the first part, Charles Chalk of the second part and Seth Chatterton of Brighton, builder of four plots of a garden site on the North East side of a new street called Southampton Street. Two pauls late Seagers and six pauls former Thomas Friends, of 64 foot long by 52 foot wide, abutting on the NW side to a messe belonging to Edwin Marwick, on the SE side to ground belonging to the said Charles Chalk, on the NE to land then or late belonging to Mr Fieldus and on the SW to the road or street called Southampton Street.

21 June 1856: Covenant by said S Chatterton, his heirs with that said C Chalk & T Wisden… that no noisy, noisome, noxious or offensive trade or business should at any time (thereafter) be carried on or permitted in or upon the said habitations at premises thereby conveyed or any part there not should anything be done or permitted in or upon the said houses which would be a nuisance or annoyance to the owners or occupiers for the time being of the adjoining land then or late of the said C Chalk…

Three houses were built on land 48 feet by 52 feet, Nos 49, 50 & 51 Southampton Street. In December 1887 Mr George Edward Mills, a coal dealer of 22 Marlborough Street bought number 50 and in 1906 bought a parcel of land situate in the rear of the premises fronting on Finsbury Road and a 10 foot roadway leading into Islingword Road on the North by an old shed and the premises lastly above described on the West by property belonging to William Smith on the East by property belonging to Reverend W Dinnick together with the stables, outhouses and premises thereon erected…

Steps were built in the back garden of number 50 Southampton Street which provided access to the yard which stables the horses and carts used in the delivery of coal. The land then contained 12 stables, four store sheds, one large cart and a large yard. The rear wall of the garden still shows the signs of the steps although they have been blocked in."

In 1870 a mortgage of £700 was taken out by Seth Chatterton with The Liberator Permanent Benefit Building Society at 6% over 12 years to purchase the property. The land at the rear of the house became the site of workshops and small factories like the pickle factory.

I lived at 61 Islingword Road as a boy in the 1920s and 30s. The Southdown Pickle Factory was at 93 and 94 Islingword Road and ran along the back of Southampton Street. The entrance was like a garage with big doors that you could drive a van through. They pickled cabbage, onions and gherkins in big jars for the trade, and there was always a strong smell of boiling vinegar. It was run by Mr Plummer who employed three people. **Gordon Harwood**

James' Dairy, on the left, is on the corner of Richmond Street and Claremont Row. Mr James is standing in the doorway of his shop. His daughter Connie is leaning against the wall waiting for her brothers to come home from Richmond Street school, on the right of the photograph

After the war the pickle factory in Islingword Road changed from pickles to beetroot and a firm called Grant Curry took it over. They had ton after ton of beetroots delivered which had to be put into sheds on the site and covered with straw and canvas, and so much would be taken into the factory each day and cooked in vats with yeast, which I think they got from the Phoenix Brewery. They then fed the yeast to the pigs, poor things.

My family were originally tallow merchants and grocers and two of my ancestors were on the committee for the railway, but later their money seemed to run out. I had two older sisters and we had a room in my grandmother's house at 8 Southampton Street where three generations lived in the same house. In 1940 we moved to No 22, and in 1942 to No 52 where we live now. My father kept chickens in the back garden and when they had to be killed I took them along to Dick Simmonds at the Charles Napier. My grandfather used to breed rabbits and sell them at Christmas because people couldn't afford a chicken.

At one time there were only local people here but when I go to the pub now I'm sometimes the only local person.

George Inman

As a child I lived at 18 Southampton Street. My father was a painter and decorator and my mother had been on the stage before she married. There were five boys and four girls in the family, so the house was crowded. It had three storeys with two rooms at street level, two rooms upstairs and two rooms downstairs. The living room was downstairs with light from a metal grating in the street. We girls slept four 'topped and tailed' to a bed. My mother would take our Sunday dinner to be baked at Hilders the bakers at 103 Islingword Road and then go to the pub with my father until it was ready.

Janet Webb

On Christmas Day, my father would take the dinners to be cooked at his bakery. They were ready to be collected at 'turning out time' at the three local pubs. Hot-cross buns were sold on Good Friday at a ha'penny each or seven buns for three pence.

The games we played were: hopscotch, biff bat, yo-yo, skipping and marbles in the gutter. Wednesday nights were 'picture nights', best seats nine pence. We went in our Austin Seven, either to The Court in New Road, The Gaiety on the Lewes Road, the Troxy at the bottom of North Road, or The Grand at the top. We were always home by 10.30 pm as my father, who was a master baker, had to make the dough. There were no machines then and he was up at five every morning.

Eve King

My mother had to work hard bringing up her brothers and sisters as her mother had died young. She would get up at 6 am, go to bed at midnight and she'd be working all day. She took in washing as well as doing all the washing for the family. She washed everything by hand in the bath, then put it through the mangle. My father did nothing.

I used to push an old pram round to the pickle factory of an evening and get two quarter hundredweight sacks of pickles and bring them home. My mother and older sister would

75

sit all evening with a big enamel bath peeling onions and putting them into bowls of water to keep cool. My mother would also be called on to assist at births and lay people out when they died. I have woken up to find three kids in my bed if their mother had died in the night. She would give us kids a list and we'd knock on every door and collect money for a wreath and any spare would be put in an envelope to help with the funeral. My mum died aged just 64, just when we were all doing well and we could have made her life so much easier.

Ron Richardson

I started working when I was 15 for Mr Jones in Edward Street who had a shop with a dairy at the back. I delivered the milk on a hand cart. When I was older and needed to be paid more, I was replaced by another young boy who would work for lower wages.

I then went to work in Preston village, where the milk was bottled in a garage, but in 1941 I joined the Co-op dairy at the bottom of Islingword Road, behind Hanover Crescent. Some of the rounds were made by hand cart and some by horse and cart. The horses were stabled at the rear of Hanover Crescent with the horses for the Co-op bakery. The bottling department was between the lane behind Hanover Crescent and the dairy; the milk was pasteurised on the top floor and was bottled, mostly by women, on the ground floor.

After the war we had electric carriers which had batteries in a box and a handle to start and stop, which was a lot easier than pushing the cart all the way to Moulsecoomb and Coldean. There was competition between the dairies and you would try to collect all the bottles you delivered but sometimes other dairies took your bottles. They used to have a collection man who would stop you to check that you didn't have bottles from other dairies. Milk was 8d a pint after the war and households were rationed to three pints a day with three quarters of a pint for children.

At one time the Co-op employed over 100 staff at Hanover Crescent and they also bought over half the houses there and used them as flats for the milkmen and their families. In 1986 the diary was taken over by the Portsmouth Co-op and they had a new depot built in Moulsecoomb Way and the Hanover Crescent depot closed. It was the end of an era for the area and for myself, as I was retired from work. It had been a hard physical job, especially in bad weather, but I have very fond memories of working there.

Frank Edwards

My father had a job with the Co-op dairy delivering milk on a hand cart and he was offered the house next door to the depot in Toronto Terrace. It was the largest house in the street and had originally been used as a laundry. All the push barrows were kept at the depot and the milk would be piled three storeys high, with eggs and butter in a little cupboard at the bottom. After the round all the milkmen had to use a hose to scrub their barrows. When my father had finished his round in the Hanover area he had to go to

London Terrace to pay in the money. It was a very heavy job because of all the hills and there were quite a few accidents with the hand carts running away. My mother said it damaged his heart and that was the reason he died young. We left Toronto Terrace after my sister became ill with diptheria and the doctors advised that the milk running from the carts into our gardens had probably caused it.

Vera Saunders

On summer evenings in the 1950s people would sit outside their front doors on upright chairs keeping an eye on the children playing in the street. If we chalked on the walls we would get a clip on the ears. Gangs of children roamed around their own territory; in icy weather we would slide down Albion Hill on tin trays. Totters with horses sold their wares, winkles and mussels were sold from a barrow on Sundays, and an Indian gentleman with a turban and a leather case sold wonderful silks. The 'Onion Johnnies' from France with their bicycles sold strings of onions.

Susan Davies

Jock Harvey, with Joe James in the delivery cart from James' dairy in Richmond Street

It used to be a stable community, our front door was always open. Now there are only three of the older people left in the street, it's mostly students and nobody stops to talk to you. We've had police breaking down a door in a drugs raid. They asked us what we wanted to see in the Community Centre but they have things like the beer festival which is not of any interest to us. Years ago the Church of the Annunciation used to have dances and we enjoyed those.

Charles and Ethel Moore

My mother's grandparents (Sebastian Indeman Brazier) lived at 5 Lewes Street in the early 1920s. All families lived near each other and didn't move away. My mother's parents lived in Grove Street and had ten children. I can remember their house with gas mantles and a black range and an outside wc with an original Victorian cistern. Everywhere smelt of lavender polish. The living room was for visitors and they kept their nice pieces in there. There was no front garden, but there was a boot scraper by the front door, and the back windows opened into a small yard. Coal was delivered and put under the stairs.
Roy Wilkinson

My mother bought bars of Sunlight soap, Monkey Brand bars and square white pumice stone-like blocks, which when dipped in cold water and rubbed on the front steps, used to dry to a dazzling white. It took some time to dry, so mum used to either have a little chat to the neighbours, or else polish the red tiles on the courtyard with Red Cardinal polish.

Goldsmith and Towner the bakers in Toronto Terrace was a lovely place; it was a wholesale bakery, but one could always go round and buy rolls from the men in the mornings. I did wonder if perhaps this was a way of putting a few more pennies in their pockets! The aroma was gorgeous, it was a lovely 'smelly' area to live in those days.
June Marshall

My mother, now 100 years old (in 1999), was the youngest daughter of nine children and lived with her parents at 46 Coleman Street – where my brother and I grew up. Her family had been very poor when she was young and she walked with my Uncle Harry to Dyke Road to the nuns to get food. I used to go to Cartwrights in New Road every week to pay the 12 shillings rent.

When trolley buses first came into use we all had a free ride around The Level. When they took up the tram lines with wooden blocks, we would buy or pinch the wood for the fire. My grandfather chopped up the blocks but they had flint in them and when they heated you heard a 'ping' and the flint would shoot out.

We used to go to the Arcadia cinema, known as 'The Scratch' in Lewes Road where the Labour Club is now. Bert the dustman was the 'chucker outer' if you were noisy, and they would come round and spray 'flit spray' which smelt foul.
Patrick Cheeseman

During the war we only went to school for half days as there were evacuees. Some of the children who came were very poor and the Brighton families had to clothe them. When the mothers came to see them they all sat in the gutters and talked to each other.
Margaret Miller

I was born in Carlyle Street, the fourth of seven children although the youngest child of my own father. My father was killed in the 1914–18 war and my mother remarried and had

78

three more children. She went out nursing the Indian troops at the Pavilion and the younger children were looked after by my mother's brothers and sisters. She rode everywhere on her bike in order to work.

There was a lot of unemployment in the 1920s and 30s, but my stepfather was a worker and would turn his hand to anything, but even he was unemployed at times. People would say that if he was out of work then there was no work to be had.

We had a bath in a half barrel, the girls on Friday night and the boys on Saturday. When I was 13 I was allowed to go to Cobden Road Baths which cost 4d. A number was given to you as you sat in a waiting room while the bath was cleaned.

There were cornfields to the left of Queen's Park Road and beside Queen's Park Pub was Chalky Lane, now Pankhurst Avenue, but there were allotments and Humphrey's farm. The Council houses were built in the 1920s.

Elm Grove was built with wooden blocks and the trams went up to the top and along Queen's Park Road from the railway works. At dinner time the trams would run from New England Road and didn't stop, so the men had to jump off and on.

Elm Grove on race days was a terrific mixture of classes, and the inmates of the workhouse were allowed to put their begging bowls or hats over the wall. I didn't think of it much when I was a kid, but it was tragic really putting out caps on string. Times were hard but the streets were safe and as children we went all over the place.
Jack Smith

Elm Grove, laying the tram lines 1901. The workhouse is on the right

*When my father married in 1919 he bought 10 Washington Street for £250. From 1905 –
1912 the house had been joined to number 9 next door and used as the Annunciation
Mission House where the Sisters of Bethany, who did a lot of good work, lived there. They
were transferred to a house in Hanover Crescent and the Church of the Annunciation sold
the houses. The church attracted people from outside the area and they would arrive in
their horse and traps, their families having long connections with the church. Number 8
Washington Street was a sort of off-licence or beer shop where you went into their front
room and they kept the barrels at the back.*

*On Good Friday when I was small, my dad would bring a scaffold rope home and all the
children would come and skip in the street. The area was more friendly when I was young,
if one was in trouble all were in trouble, and they would give you their last crust of bread.
Now a lot of people don't speak to each other. There are only three of the original families
left in the street.*
Betty Bergin

Hanover is now a fashionable town centre residential area, previously popular with first
time buyers, but is now occupied by professional families and students.

***Mr J Nicholas and Miss M Burden, Acting Master and Matron of the Poor Law
Institution in Elm Grove, known as the Brighton Workhouse in 1911***

Shops

Hanover was probably self-sufficient in shops in the 1930s so daily life could be led in this compact area. Everything could be found here, homes, extended families, friends, schools, shops, churches and chapels. Sadly very few shops now remain.

J C Archer and his 'boy' Stuart Johnson

My grandfather Jesse Archer moved to Brighton to open the Sainsbury's shop in St James's Street; he planned to build up trade and open his own shop, hoping to take some of their trade. He leased a shop in Richmond Buildings and many of his customers came with him. He wore a blue serge long dress coat with white cuffs, and later he wore a white coat, apron, shirt sleeves and a straw hat, or a white coat and a trilby. In the 1930s there was no refrigeration, so ice boxes were used, the ice being delivered every two weeks. During the war my grandfather sheltered in the ice box during the air raids. He would sometimes leave his shop unattended while he went for a drink in the Lennox Arms opposite, but his customers always knew where he was and called in at the pub to ask to be served. His customers were loyal to him and he treated them well. During the war when the men came home on leave he would allow the women extra rations.

Richmond Buildings being demolished 1954. New building is going up in Ashton Street

After the war Richmond Buildings became part of a Slum Clearance Area and one by one the shops closed. My grandfather was one of the last to leave as he refused the shop they offered him in Richmond Parade, as he felt the community would take time to build up again. He finally moved to 128 Islingword Road where the shop is today. My grandfather died soon afterwards.

From the age of eight I helped in the shop, skinning rabbits and turning the sausage machine. Sometimes I went to the meat market in Russell Street to help select the meat which was delivered by carrier. In the 1960s there were 12 butchers in the area, but with the growth of the supermarkets small shops closed. The BSE scare caused trade to drop even more and we decided to deal only in organic meat and buy directly from farms. This has improved our trade and more people are turning away from the supermarkets and rediscovering the small butcher.

Brian Archer

The Cook Shop, 135 Islingword Road

My great-grandmother Frances Ladd (1850–1936) opened a cook shop at 135 Islingword Road. She had 22 live births in 23 years but only 11 children survived, and they all helped with the business as they grew older, especially the girls. They went to the slaughterhouse and bought the offal, sheep and cows' heads, and boned them for the brains, tongue and flesh on the cheek. The meat pies were made with scraps and kidneys and the cooking was done in big ovens housed in the backyard. New potatoes would be swilled around in a barrel with a besom broom because they were easier to peel than old potatoes. They grew their own sage and onion for the pies in their own greenhouses. The family would not eat their own produce but would buy joints of beef from Mr Warner, the butcher next door.

Benjamin and Frances Ladd on their silver wedding at Islingword Place c1895

The shop was successful and Frances bought 11 Islingword Road and the coal yard opposite with the profits. They kept the barrow used for collecting the meat in the coal yard and employed a boy, called Tom, to come straight from school and assist them with the heavier work. They started to bag up the coal in small bags and sell it at the cookshop, there was just enough coal in each bag for one night. Later my grandmother Edith Sully and her husband took over the cookshop.

Sonia Waterton

F J Harman, greengrocers, 137 Islingword Road

My father owned the greengrocer's at 137 Islingword Road for over 40 years. He went to the market at Black Lion Street every Tuesday and Saturday and opened seven days a week, Sunday until after lunch. He closed weekdays at about 6pm but if there was trade still about he would stay open. He bought some of his produce from Henfield, and Worthing tomatoes graded with different coloured paper. He sold firewood and coal and did some removals too.

Arthur Harman

Rackman's grocery shop at 32 Richmond Buildings

We moved to Brighton in the early 1930s and my stepfather rented a grocery shop at 32 Richmond Buildings for 30 shillings per week, and we lived above it. There were other grocers in the street and he really didn't make a good living. My stepfather felt that he had been misled as to the trade he might expect. The shop was open from 7.30 am – 6 pm every day except Sunday when we closed at 1 pm. We weren't allowed to sell groceries on a Sunday, only cigarettes and firewood.

The shop was opposite the Lennox Arms and on Friday and Saturday night when I went up to the cold attic to bed with just a candle for light, I would enjoy the piano playing and singing coming from the bar. During the war it was my job to cut out all the coupons, count them and send them to the Ministry of Food, my stepfather didn't like doing it as it was so fiddly.

John Rackman

Grocery shop at 102 Richmond Street, Brighton

In 1952 we were looking for a small grocery shop and found 102 Richmond Street at a reasonable rent. Brighton Council informed us by letter that no development plan for the area was likely in the next 20 years. We moved in during 1952, but imagine our dismay when in 1953 Brighton Council published a plan for redevelopment of the area of our shop. I think it was probably two years before the clearance started, but after that we saw surrounding houses knocked down with nothing to replace them. We knew one family with two young children who had bought their little terraced house with a mortgage, and spent a lot of money improving it, who were given £5 for their property, which was what most people received. We were more fortunate as the new lease, the letter and the low rent enabled us to claim all we spent on the property. Gradually all our customers were moved to areas on the edge of the town.

When we arrived food was still rationed and we had several new customers who registered with us. I think the butter and cheese rations were only 2oz per person per week. Biscuits were weighed into bags from large tins with glass lids and sliced bread had just started.

Our main wholesalers were Button's in Cheltenham Place and Gravett's at the bottom of Trafalgar Street. Gravett's sold mostly tinned foods, but Button's sold bacon and a wide range of foods. At one time they offered us some 10lb tins of German ham and as we had just bought a slicer we decided to try it. This was a great success and people came from all over the place just for the ham. At Christmas time people would order bacon joints and we would buy sides of bacon which we cut up to order. We sold cigarettes and we split the packets and let people have one or two at a time as this was all they could afford. We didn't have much trouble with bad debts although we did have a 'book', but people mainly settled every week, which we tried to insist on.

We had no refrigerator but the cellar stayed the same temperature all year round. One very hot summer we had to keep our butter down there, which we weighed out in two and four ounce packs, this meant we had to go up and down the stairs, so we bought a cool box, but it grew mould inside. We also sold bundles of chopped firewood. We weighed dried fruit, split peas, lentils, rice, etc, and older people will remember the blue paper which came in squares, which the grocer had to fold into a cone shape, called a 'poke'.
Betty Parsons

Butcher's Shop at 83 Southover Street, Brighton

My father William Cheesman started working in the shop when he was 20 years old. I think it had always been a butcher's shop and they originally slaughtered the animals at the rear. From the age of 12 I helped my father, mostly with deliveries, because people didn't have refrigerators then and liked to have their meat fresh on Saturdays, when my father worked from 6 am – 5 pm.

The meat came from the Russell Street abattoir but later it transferred to Hollingdean Road. We went on Mondays to select meat and anything big was delivered, but if we needed something urgently we would go any day. My father would stay up all night for two or three days before Christmas trussing the birds and, as there was no refrigeration, it was hoped that they would all sell. On Christmas Day my father would be ill as a result.

After the Second World War trade was good in the Southover Street area, we had very loyal customers who could buy everything they wanted in the street. At the time there were three butchers, three boot repairers, three barbers, three newsagents, one laundry, four greengrocers, two chemists – Mr O'Flinn had one at the top of the street and his wife had

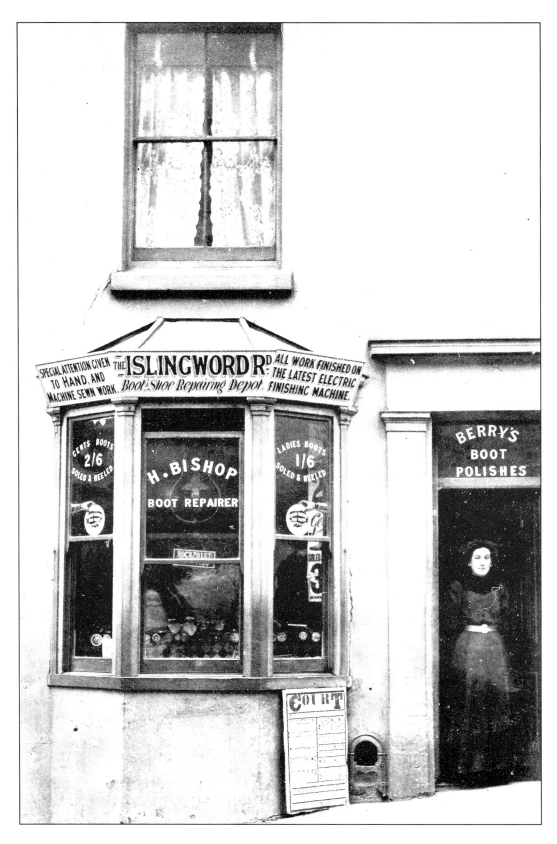

one at the bottom – and six or seven grocers who also sold hardware. There were many pubs on street corners and along the adjoining streets. Trade began to change about 20 years ago with the development of the supermarkets. For 10 years trade didn't go down but didn't improve, but during the last 10 years trade has gone down. My mother still lived above the shop and was burgled one night and all the meat was stolen, so we decided to sell. The shop has now been converted into a house, as many other shops have been.
Michael Cheesman

The Misses Carter had a sweet shop in Albion Hill where you could buy ice cream or a cone of jelly for a ha'penny. They made all their own toffee and in late summer they would pick the apples from the tree in the back garden for toffee apples. When there were no apples left they would twist the toffee around a stick. They would also melt bars of chocolate and put peanuts in it and call them 'nut brittles'. Unfortunately the shop was bombed during the war and never reopened.
Jackie Griffiths

Ada Wood had a sweet shop opposite Grove Street which sold sweets and odds and ends, there were mice running all over the stock in the window. At 15 Southover Street there was an old bootmaker, Mr Wood, who would always be in his window, with nails in his mouth as he worked.
Roy Wilkinson

Miss Foote lived with her elderly mother at 75 Southover Street, and ran a toy shop. We only remember the little toys, evil tin pea-shooters that cut your lips to ribbons and nearly choked you if you breathed in the dried peas instead of blowing; penny whistles, yo-yos, hoops, matchboxes with surprises such as tiny metal puzzles, the smallest wooden or china dolls, tiny jig-saws, playing cards, biff-bats, mouth organs – which gave out awful noises and cut you to bits. My favourite was a soft ball on elastic covered with stockinette and decorated in red, blue and silver cottons.

Miss Foote had another string to her bow, she was a music teacher, and on Saturday mornings held piano and violin lessons. We didn't have a piano at the time, so the resourceful Miss Foote devised a paper keyboard which we had to practise on.
June Marshall

I grew up in Grove Street in the 1950s when there was still rationing. Locally we would shop at Tuppen's where you could get the broken bits of the bacon and Hudson's who sold vinegar from barrels. If we went to the big shops in London Road it would be to Woolworth's with their very large wooden counters, or Sainsbury's towards Preston Circus, where you had to queue at every counter.
Susan Davies

Opposite: Henry Bishop boot repairer 10 Islingword Road, 1908—1954

C Biddleston, 4 Islingword Road, hardware shop 1934–35

90

As you entered Haine's the grocers on the corner of Beaufort Terrace you were engulfed by the smell of Sunlight soap mixed with that of the biscuits and raisins, bacon and cheese.
Janice Ravenett

I was born at 22 Montreal Road. My mother always shopped locally, she went to Southwell's, a butcher in Southover Street. I would be sent with a list of the meat for the week and it was delivered by a boy on a bike. Mum always insisted on one and a half pounds of the 10 penny steak, rather than the 8 pence per pound, because they threw in a kidney. We belonged to the Christmas club there where we saved all year for a big piece of pork, never chicken – we didn't know what chicken tasted like. Mr West the grocer, on the corner of Albion Hill and Montreal Road, sold most things and you could weigh out your own sugar and tea and watch butter being patted out. Mr Collins from Quebec Street came round with his greengrocery barrow, but it was only a front because he took bets. The fishermen also came round selling from their barrows.

The draper's shop in Montreal Road became a launderette and the baker's shop at the bottom of the road has become an estate agent. I loved walking by Puttock's the baker's shop on the way to and from school because of the lovely smell of bread. You could buy yesterday's bread and cakes cheaply, most of us went home for lunch so I would sometimes buy myself a cheap cake.
Olive Denman [Olive Denman lived at 22 Montreal Road until the end of her life.]

I was born in Montreal Road in 1926. There were a lot of shops in Islingword Road, the pawnbrokers at No 43 was run by Mr Dorey, and my mother, who loved a bargain, bought quite a lot of good class things there, including a canteen of cutlery. My uncle had a butcher's shop at 123 Islingword Road which has recently been made into a house.
E Campbell

On Saturday night there used to be a market on The Level, which was under canvas and had flares for lighting. My mother would send me down with seven shillings and tell me to wait until I heard seven shillings and bought the meat. It used to be enormous and I had difficulty carrying it up Southover Street.
Dorothy Farrell

I lived at 24 Windmill Street during the 1920s and 30s. My mother shopped locally but also used St James's Street because it was cheaper and you could buy broken biscuits and dried peas that were already soaked. On the corner of Montreal Road there was a bakers and every Saturday afternoon my mother would make a large cake and take it to be baked for sixpence.
Edna Dray

Opposite: 57a Richmond Street on the corner of Windmill Terrace. Frederick and Ada Hills outside their shop with two of their staff c1914. Converted to a house in the 1960s

Hanover Herald

Eve King moved to Brighton in the 1920s when she was six years old and lived most of her life at 17 Southover Street. Eve's father was a master baker with a shop on the corner of Coleman Street. At the lower end of Southover Street was a row of small cottages with a touch of countryside. On entering a huge oak door it was like walking into a fairytale – a long garden path flanked with flowers, shrubs, trees and greenhouses. At the end of the path was a lovely farmhouse where you could get butter, eggs and jams and everything smelled delicious.

Payne's milk and greengroceries were delivered by horse and cart. The horse would mount the pavement and come to our shop door for bits. Southover Street was always a dangerous hill, and many times horse carts and lorries delivering beer lost control. I remember that Clarke's Brewery had a horse and cart, and the driver would turn out of Belgrave Street down into Coleman Street; the poor horse would be terrified. One day the cart, driver and horse slithered down the hill and crashed into a lamppost at the corner of Hanover Terrace. A traction engine which delivered flour to our side bakehouse door also came to the same fate. His brakes failed and the traction engine ended up in the wall of the laundry at the corner of Hanover Street.

I was born above my parents' shop, which sold groceries and milk, at 94 Richmond Street on the corner of Claremont Row. I was the sixth of eight children, five boys and three girls and my mother stopped working in the shop after I was born. When my father became ill he sold many of the rounds off to the men who worked for him.
Connie Dowds

You could get everything you wanted in Richmond Buildings and it stayed open until the 'devil's dancing hours'. Mrs Smith on the corner of Hanover Terrace sold everything; if she didn't have it in she'd get it for you.
Kathleen Lilley

Dorey's pawnshop was on the corner of Islingword Road. I remember wearing my best suit for visiting relatives and being told not to get anything down it because it was going back into pawn. We pawned our sheets and blankets when times were hard and slept with our overcoats on.
Albert Saunders

Dolly Rogers had a pease pudding and faggot shop in Islingword Road and she gave piano lessons upstairs.
Margaret Miller

Most industrial cities consist of loosly defined villages, Hanover was one of Brighton's villages and was almost self-contained with its collections of shops, schools, churches, chapels and public houses.

The corner shop keeper played and important role in advising her customers on matters such as illnesses and discipline, knowledge which had been gleaned from other customers. Gossip, the prime leisure activity, but also the purveyor of knowledge and advice, played an important part in a community which relied almost entirely on the spoken word.

Now the car and the supermarket have destroyed the network of all but a few, local shops, and most of them have now been converted to houses. Without the local shops not so many people walk about the streets, meet each other, or watch out for each other and get to know their neighbours.

The metal box on wheels is a great isolater.

ENDPIECE

The Hanover described in this book has long gone. Its character has changed, its population has changed and its houses have changed. But some things have remained through all the shifting sands of the past seventy years.

From being an area where in the 1920s it was reputed that the police patrolled in fours it has become a desirable area to live, particularly if you are young and sociable. The poverty and the sense of restricted life have gone, as have the corner shop and the even more common corner public house. Takeaways now dot the streets, along with a smattering of specialist shops like an organic butcher and an eco-friendly undertaker, run by women. The churches, chapels and schools that marked the old life are now largely upmarket housing.

The residents are different nowadays. From being largely tenants of poor housing the years after World War Two saw the Welfare State improving the lot of the many and houses began to be bought rather than rented. But the big change was in the sixties when young academics from the new University of Sussex were attracted by the low house prices and good transport links to Falmer. Nowadays it has become more of a student base, intermingled with the long-time residents who continue to live there.

Gone are the outside lavatories and the bread ovens. Gone too the drab unpainted render of the old streets. Most houses have been massively improved internally, partially due to the General Improvement Area status in the seventies. The streets show a kaleidoscope of paint colours as owner-occupiers express their individuality.

But one thing that has not gone is the sense of community. The old inhabitants were united in poverty and so built up strong networks of mutual support. Surprisingly the influx of a very different type of resident only served to emphasise this sense of community. From their joint efforts came a newspaper which has developed into a book publisher, a Community Centre with a very active programme and an annual street Festival that is one of the best in Brighton. It is also a hub of music, the home of a surprising number of Brighton bands.

Hanover today is one of the most distinctive parts of Brighton. To walk its streets gives a feeling that is different to the rest of the city. It has a fizz, a buzz, a liveliness and a sense of community that sets it apart. Hanover is Hanover, and not Brighton.

The old Hanover has been recreated by listening to residents who knew that earlier life, who knew the richness of their social relationships and the adversities of insecure and underpaid employment. We can sample the current Hanover, and only wonder at the degree of change.

Derek Burns

94

LIST OF STREETS

Italics indicate those streets now demolished

1809–20	*Ashton Street, Richmond Buildings & Terrace, Apollo Terrace, Claremont Street & Row, Ivory Place,* Richmond Street & Gardens
1809–21	Albion Hill, Waterloo Place, Phoenix Place, Richmond Terrace
1821–30	*Cambridge Street*
1822–30 & 1865-69	Southover Street (previously a turnpike road)
1848–53	Newhaven Street
1854–58	Milton Road, Windmill Street
1859–64	*Dinapore Street, Liverpool Street*
1859–64	Howard, Hampton, Southampton, Jersey, Belgrave & Lewes Streets, Cobden Road, Islingword Road & Place
1865–69	Islingword Street, Finsbury Road, Toronto Terrace, Montreal Road, Quebec Street, Scotland Street, Holland Street and Whichelo Place
1870–74	Stanley Street
1875–79	Beaufort Terrace
1880–84	Elm Grove, Luther, Bentham, Carlyle, Arnold, Lynton, Baxter, Cromwell, Grant, Jackson & Lincoln Streets
1890–99	Ewart & Grove Streets, Windmill Terrace
1931	Elmore & Tarner Roads, Tilbury Way

Interviews by Jacqueline Pollard ©

Interviews in order of their appearance in the first edition:

Betty Parker, Robert Gregory, G Haywood, Susan Davies, E Campbell, Walter Hope, Pamela Sprinthall, Gordon Harwood, June Marshall, Olive Denman, J Fennel, F E Smith, P Brooker, Connie Dowds, Olive Pelling, Bernard Pelling, Betty Gillett, Vera Saunders, Michael Evans, Derek Nelmes, Sonia Waterton, Dennis Alderson, Eve King, Jackie Griffiths, Kathleen Lilley, Roy Wilkinson, John Rackham, Frank Edwards, Patrick Cheeseman, Margaret Miller, Dorothy Farrell, Charles Moore, Harriett Waldron, Betty Ticehurst, Roseann West, Ralph Howard, Daphne Howard, Janet Webb, George Inman, Ron Richardson, Albert Pattenden, Susan Davies, Charles Moore, Ethel Moore, Roy Wilkinson, June Marshall, Betty Bergin, Arthur Harman, John Rackman, Betty Parsons, Michael Cheeseman, Janice Ravenett, Olive Denman, Edna Dray, Kathleen Lilley, Albert Saunders, Margaret Miller.

Without whom this book could not have been made.

ACKNOWLEDGEMENTS

Historical research: Jacqueline Pollard and Lavender Jones
Interviews: © Jacqueline Pollard
Design, additional text and editing: Selma Montford
Photographic research: Jacqueline Pollard and Peter Booth
Maps: Lavender Jones
Teaching and technical support: Computer Box
Typing; Alice Elliott

Photographs
Many of the photographs are reproduced from the J S Gray collection with the kind permission of the Regency Society of Brighton & Hove. The collection of 39 volumes is at present in the process of being digitised. The photographs which have already been digitised can be viewed on the Regency Society's website www.regencysociety.org. The Society invites sponsorship for volumes still to be digitised. Credit is given to all sponsors on the website. Brighton Books Publishing has sponsored one of the four volumes on the Old Town. Contact: Duncan McNeill 01273 504654 for details of sponsorship,

Peter Booth, Brighton Museum, Chris Horlock, Frank Edwards, Robert Jeeves of 'Step Back in Time', Brian Archer, Connie Dowd and Jacqueline Pollard loaned photographs. Some of the photographs have been reproduced with the assistance of Yiorgos Nikiteas. John Holwell allowed us to reproduce his late wife's grandmother Emily Simm's sampler.

Information from: Brian Archer; Christopher Beaumont; David Beevers, Keeper of Fine Art at Brighton Museum; Kate Bujama; Joyce Collins; Barry Hewland; Peter Holtham; Colin Jones; Jane Launchbur; Henry Smith; Barbara de Souza and Father David Worstenholm.

References: 'Churches of Brighton' by J. Sawyer c1880; 'Encyclopaedia of Brighton' by Timothy Carder, East Sussex County Libraries, 1990; 'The Brighton Blitz' by David Rowland; 'A Peep into the Past' by J G Bishop, Brighton Herald Office 1880.

Hilly Laine to Hanover : a Brighton Neighbourhood was first published in 1999
ISBN 1-901454-04-5 This edition Hilly Laine to Hanover : a Brighton Neighbourhood
2008 edition; ISBN 978-1-901454-11-6 published by Brighton Books Publishing
10 Clermont Road Brighton BN1 6SG
tel: 01273-509209 fax: 01273-502018 email: info@brightonbooks.co.uk
website: www.brightonbooks.co.uk blog:brightonbooks.wordpress.com

Printed by Delta Press, Unit 1, Industrial House, Conway Street, Hove BN3 3LW